the Miracle

the Miracle

SIX STEPS TO ENLIGHTENMENT

DR. JOE VITALE

Hypnotic Marketing, Inc.

WIMBERLEY, TX

Copyright © 2016 by Joe Vitale

All rights reserved. No part of this publication may be reproduced, distributed or transmitted in any form or by any means, including photocopying, recording, or other electronic or mechanical methods, without the prior written permission of the author or publisher, except in the case of brief quotations embodied in critical reviews and certain other noncommercial uses permitted by copyright law. For more information, please contact support@mrfire.com, or write:

Hypnotic Marketing, Inc.
PO Box 2924
Wimberley, TX 78676
www.JoeVitale.com

This publication is designed to provide accurate and authoritative information with regard to the subject matter covered. It's sold with the understanding that the author and publisher are not engaged in rendering legal, intellectual property, accounting, medical, psychological, or other professional advice. If legal advice or other professional assistance is required, the services of a competent professional should be sought. Dr. Joe Vitale and Hypnotic Marketing, Inc. individually or corporately, do not accept any responsibility for any liabilities resulting from the actions of any parties involved.

Cover design: Ted Angel
Editing and interior design: Tanya Brockett, www.HallagenInk.com

The Miracle/Joe Vitale.—1st ed.

To my late Mother, with gratitude and love.

There are only two ways to live your life. One is as though nothing is a miracle. The other is as though everything is a miracle.

—ALBERT EINSTEIN

CONTENTS

Foreword .... *xi*
Prelude .... *xvii*
Acknowledgements .... *xxi*
Author's Introduction... *xxiii*

STEP ONE: The Missing Secret 1
STEP TWO: The RAS Intention 49
STEP THREE: Counterintention Clearing 109
STEP FOUR: Einstein's Secret 155
STEP FIVE: Expect Miracles...................................... 201
STEP SIX: The Awakening... 243

Bonus Material: Inner Child Meditation.................... *285*
Bibliography.. *291*
About the Author.. *295*
Special Miracles Coaching® Offer *297*

By Susan Shumsky, D.D.

Foreword

I first met Joe Vitale when he invited me to speak at his "Miracles Weekend" in San Diego. I would describe Joe with four words: sincerity, integrity, authenticity, and passion. Joe is the real deal, folks. This is a man whose passion is to uplift people in every way he can conceive. He is highly creative and therefore is continually inspired to generate new ways to help people achieve their full potential. That is why, when Joe asked me to write a foreword for this book, *The Miracle*, I was happy to study the book, use its methods for myself (with excellent results), and write about it.

My background is in Eastern wisdom and New Thought. I spent twenty-two years in the ashrams of Maharishi Mahesh Yogi, the guru of the Beatles and guru of Deepak Chopra. Seven of those years I served on Maharishi's personal staff. Then I studied and taught New Thought for another twenty-eight years through my self-empowerment program Divine Revelation©. I am a best-selling, award-winning author of thirteen books, including *Miracle Prayer*, *Instant Healing*, *Divine Revelation*, and *Awaken Your Divine Intuition*.

Undoubtedly you have some idea of what it means to study with a guru from India. But what the heck is this "New Thought" I am referring to, which Joe Vitale often mentions in his books? Well, it is the fundamental philosophy that *The Secret* and *The Attractor Factor* are based upon. All motivational speakers and sales trainers, from Napoleon Hill and Norman Vincent Peale to Louise Hay and Les Brown, use its principles.

New Thought, a nonsectarian philosophy with no formal creed, proposes: 1) We cause and create everything internally through our own minds, 2) The remedy for all defect and disorder is mental and spiritual, 3) God is indwelling Spirit, and we are all children of God, and 4) Life is crowned with joy, health, and abundance. New Thought teachings were developed by such illumined souls as Phineas Parkhurst Quimby (1802–1866): miraculous healer; Ernest Holmes (1887–1960): founder of Centers for Spiritual Living and author of *The Science of Mind*; and Charles (1854–1948) and Myrtle (1845–1931) Fillmore: co-founders of the Unity Church.

Yet the roots of New Thought lie in antiquity, in the ancient scriptures of the Far East. Yes, it is true that "The Secret" is not a new secret. In the very first verse of the first chapter of the primary Buddhist scripture, the *Dhammapada*, Buddha says: *"All that we are is the result of what we have thought."* Let us pause for a moment to take this in, because it is a stunning statement. "ALL that we are," not some of what we are, not occasionally what we are, not what we are every other Tuesday, but "ALL THAT WE ARE is the result of what we have thought."

This is what Joe Vitale is telling us in *The Miracle*. He shows us that we create our own destiny through our thoughts, words, and actions. And with Ho'oponopono, Joe teaches us that we are one hundred percent responsible, not only for our own lives, but for everyone and everything around us. This is difficult to wrap our heads around and tough to accept. Because we say, "But I didn't want to attract this illness." "But I didn't want my husband to leave me." "But I didn't want my business to fail." "But I didn't want this. I didn't create this suffering."

The reality is that our conscious mind and ego did *not* create this. Our subconscious mind *did*. Our conscious beliefs are what we *think* we believe. Our subconscious beliefs are what we *really* believe. So it is our subconscious beliefs that create our destiny. These deepest subconscious beliefs "outpicture" or "demonstrate" (that means they show up) in our life.

People ask me, "How do I discover what's in my unconscious mind?" The answer is simple: Just look at your life. Whatever your deepest unconscious beliefs are, that is what your life experience is right now. So if you really believe you are wealthy, healthy, happy, and fulfilled, or poor, unhealthy, unhappy, and discontent, that is exactly what you are.

Solomon tells us, *"For as he thinketh in his heart, so is he."* Jesus says, *"As thou hast believed, so be it done unto thee."* Henry Ford declares, *"If you believe that you can do a thing, or if you believe that you cannot, you are right."* Ralph Waldo Emerson says, *"Once you make a decision, the universe conspires to make it happen."* Joe Vitale tells us, *"We live in a belief driven universe. Change your beliefs and you get a different universe."*

These "beliefs" referred to by some of the greatest minds of all time are our deepest unconscious convictions, not the random thoughts passing through our conscious minds, not the list of goals that we wrote in our journal or pasted on our vision boards, and not the intentions of our egos.

In *The Miracle*, Joe helps us unearth the cause behind our deepest unconscious beliefs and shows us how to transform them. He offers several practical, hands-on processes for overcoming counterintentions. He teaches many methods for manifesting what we want to have, do, or be. He teaches us the difference between intentions and inspirations and how to live an inspired life. He helps us create and live miracles every day. He shows us how we can be enlightened. This book is a complete guide to materialization through our own mighty power of thought, visualization, affirmation, and inspired action.

Joe takes us through four stages: victimhood, empowerment, surrender/co-creation, and finally awakening/merging with divinity. On this journey, we discover: We are not victims; we are volunteers. Nothing ever happens "to us"; we only happen to ourselves. The bad news is that we created everything ourselves—bad because we cannot blame anyone else for our problems. The good news is that we created everything ourselves—good because we can change our destiny, and even the destiny of others around us. And ultimately, we can create anything, even spiritual awakening and enlightenment. In this book *The Miracle*, Joe Vitale shows us how.

> *"Whosoever…shall not doubt in his heart, but shall believe that those things which he saith shall come to pass; he shall have whatsoever he saith." —Jesus*

—Susan Shumsky, D.D.

Dr. Susan Shumsky is an award-winning, best-selling author of eleven books, a foremost spirituality expert, a highly-acclaimed and greatly respected professional speaker, and she has decades of experience as an educator in the consciousness field.
http://www.divinerevelation.org/

By Dee Wallace

Prelude

When Joe asked me to write the prelude for his new book, *The Miracle: Six Steps to Enlightenment*, I thought, "Why me?" In that automatic question was the answer that represents why ***everyone*** should read this book. Why not me? What are the thought processes that led to the response, "Why me?" instead of the response, "Of course me!"? I believe that those of us on the sincere path of self-responsibility are at this turning point right now.

I have an integrity issue that will not allow me to endorse anything without reading it. It has to be a truthful response from my heart. I know, as an actress, that you can "act" it, or you can "be" it, and I believe the audience always knows the difference.

Thank God I read this book. It puts together all the options and tools available for us to shift into passionate power. The message is shared simply and with repetition so that you get it over and over again, and this is essential to having your brain take ownership. Joe also has this magical way of saying things so simply that you feel like you're sitting down and having a great discussion over a glass of wine. It's available. He's available. The information is available.

I finished this book with so many great, expansive ahas, and I knew what to do to implement his teachings. It took a while because I really involved myself in the exercises, and in the thought processes, and I allowed myself to shift...substantially. In simple ways, this book reached even deeper into the recesses of my subconscious and helped me retrain my brain so I am an integrated whole within myself.

I teach conscious creation. Daily. I am always searching for material that can expand me. I found it in this book. Even if you have heard the concepts before, Joe has a way of presenting them in new, understandable ways. You are going to love this book. Especially if you take the time to really do the explorations. The opening quote stopped me for two days while I explored and mined the gold within.

Joe has a great love and reverence for The Divine, the Creative Force, God, The Universe. You can feel his partnership with it, which blesses him with the undeniable power of co-creation. If it is time for you to be at peace with The Divine again, in a whole new conceptual definition, you will feel yourself back to that place of grace in these pages. You will feel the love. That's what Joe is. Love. And he teaches it well. Welcome to "The Miracle." It's You!

—Dee Wallace

Dee Wallace is a Hollywood actress, the author of five books on self-creation, a channeler of healing work, a radio host of her own weekly show, a sought out speaker, and she has appeared on every major news and talk show including E!, True Hollywood Stories, Oprah, *and* The O'Reilly Factor.
https://iamdeewallace.com/

Acknowledgements

As always, creating a book is a group effort. I want to thank Vishen Lakhiani for inviting me to create an original definitive course for his MindValley company, which became the foundation for this book. Tanya Brockett of Hallagen Ink edited the course into book form and helped clarify the content. Suzanne Burns and Zion Chatele have been with me a long time, as friends and assistants, without whom few of my projects would get done, including this one. Ted Angel created the beautiful cover, which I think is a "clearing" tool all by itself. The team at Achieve Today, who runs my Miracles Coaching® program, are all beautiful souls who help carry my work into the world. And of course, Nerissa, my love, is always there for me. I love you all and thank you all. I am grateful.

Author's Introduction

I am so grateful that you have joined me here for *The Miracle: Six Steps to Enlightenment*. I believe that this book contains the best that I have to offer to date. It is the culmination of decades of learning, application, sharing, and teaching that I have done. It is a very important work that will allow you to not only determine what it is you want to create, but it will also help you to clear the path for that creation and the reception of that manifestation. The steps you take in this book will help you to open up the channels for making real everything you have been wanting for so long.

You know, since my appearance in *The Secret*, I have been asked on a regular basis, "How is it that you are able to make so many things happen? You manifest cars, you manifest wealth, you manifest books, movies, and music CDs. How is it that you are able to manifest all of those things when I can't even get my monthly rent paid?"

The answer is found on these pages. The answer is found in opening yourself up and clearing your channels to receive everything that you are looking to gain. If you have ever asked, "what are those things that I need to do so I can be clear to receive like you do?" Those answers are the *Six Steps to Enlightenment*. Through all of the exercises that I provide, and all the meditations that I guide you through, you will be able to make *The Miracle* real in your own life, on a continuous basis.

So it is my expectation that this book is going to take you places you've never been before. This book is going to help you to do more than you ever have before. It is going to help you to clear more out of your life—more baggage, more deadweight, more negativity—than you've ever cleared before, so you can be open to receive, be open to connect with the Divine, and be open to take those *Six Steps to Enlightenment* and expect a true awakening in your own life.

Expect miracles.

STEP ONE

The Missing Secret

The meaning you give an event is actually the belief that attracted the event.

—Joe Vitale

What would it mean for you to have miracles in your life every day? How would you approach each morning if you knew that miracles were always on your calendar?

Welcome to *The Miracle: Six Steps to Enlightenment*. Thanks for joining me. I'm glad to be here because we're going to do something historic. This is going to be a defining moment in your life. This is something that's going to change everything. What I mean by that is you may have read some of my books, you may have seen the movie *The Secret*, or you may have taken other courses, but what I want to give you is the definitive transformation. I want to create with you an entire program that is going to change your life forever.

Been There, Done That

I don't care where you are. I don't care what you're struggling with. I've been there. We've all struggled. I've definitely struggled but I've transcended. I've come out to the other side. So with your help, what we're going to do here together is create a miracle. The miracle called your life. This whole book is based on a six-step path to enlightenment called *The Miracle*, but by the time we are done, you're going to be living the miracle.

This is going to be something that you will reflect on as being the greatest investment of your life; the greatest investment of you. You may have read my books; you may have listened to some of my audios. That's all good, that's a foundation, but where I'm sitting right now goes beyond everything else I've ever done. What I want to share with you is more than I've ever written about.

What I want to share with you is material, secrets, tips, and insights that are going to unlock the inner you. It's going to help you tear down the blocks, the unseen blocks as well as the seen blocks. We're going to do that together and I'm going to hold your hand as we go through all of this so it's going to be easy and it's going to be effortless. I do ask you to show up and be mentally ready each time you pick up this book. I do ask that you participate. I do ask that you reflect on everything every day through these six steps and do whatever is asked of you.

It's not going to be a big deal. I'm not asking you to climb mountains or anything, but I am asking you to look within, because as Carl Jung said, "Who looks outside, dreams; who looks inside, awakes." We're going to look inside and together we're going to awaken.

I have shared this material with people from Australia, Greece, Spain, London, Switzerland, Africa, and the United States. It has been all over the world, which is amazing. I'm very flattered that now you have made time to spend with me through this book.

What Do You Want to Create?

What I want to do here is to ask you to pick something that you would like to have, do, or be. What I mean by that is I want you to pretend that you can have anything. If I can wave a magic wand and give you anything that you can name, what would you like to have? You see, I want you to choose something now. You can change it later if you want. You can refine it later as you want. As we go through these six steps, we're going to perfect everything. We're going to polish everything.

You'll have new insights and you might change your mind about what you want, but because I want this to be practical, I want you to be able to use this and not just make it something that's fun or something that's entertaining for you. What I want you to do is actually take this to the bank. I want you to be able to reflect on this and say, "This was a turning point in my life. When I read that book by Joe Vitale called *The Miracle*, I chose a miracle and I saw it come to be."

You'll likely have more than one desire to manifest, but you're going to learn the basic techniques with one, so you can then apply it to others. We're going to go beyond what everybody else teaches here and we're going to transcend all of that so you can truly have virtually anything you could imagine, but we need to start someplace. So I want you to start with one thing that you pick now.

What if I Don't Know What I Want?

Some people tell me they don't know what to pick, or they don't know what they want. The first thing I will tell you is to just make it up. Just have fun. For the purposes of this book, pick something out of the sky. Just pull it down and say this is what you want. If you need further help, what I often do is a prosperity exercise. I tell people to pretend that they're going to win the lottery. In mid-2015 in the United States, for example, the lottery was up to over a hundred million dollars. That's a lot of money.

I am not encouraging you to gamble. I am not encouraging you to play the lottery and I'm not encouraging you to buy a ticket. I am encouraging you to use this as a prosperity exercise. Imagine if you won $100 million dollars tonight and even after taxes you go home with, we'll say $50 million dollars in cash. What would you do? Yes, I know you're going to buy a new car. Yes, I know you're going to buy shoes and clothes, and you're going to travel around the world, and you're going to do wonderful things. You're going to give money to worthy causes. That's all great.

When the dust settles and you wake up one morning on the beach, what are you going to do then? What are you going to do with your life at that point? That's what I want you to think about. I know people who have become extremely wealthy, but they don't sit around and loaf. What they do is take a little time off and then they decide, "Oh, I've always wanted to do..." [fill in the blank]. That's what I want you to be thinking about. What do you want to have, do, or be?

Another way to look at this is to pretend that you're a child again. When you were a child, what did you want to be, what did you want to have, what did you want to experience? When you were a child, you weren't thinking about what was impossible. You weren't thinking about limitations. You were thinking *I'm going to be an astronaut*. You were thinking you were going to be a driver of a fire engine. You were thinking all kinds of things. What comes to mind now?

Another way to come up with ideas is to look at your hobbies. If you chose a hobby and you would do it whether you got paid or not, what would it be? All of this is around the idea of selecting one thing to work on as you go through this book.

Again, you can have other goals. You can have other intentions. You can want to attract or attain anything that you like, but we want to start with one. So I invite you to write that down right now—whatever came to mind—and if you're struggling with it a little bit, make it up.

Examples might be that you want to feel happier, you want to date more, you want to lose weight, or you want to gain weight. You want more money, you want more sales, you want a relationship, you want a different job, or you want a different house. It doesn't matter. Make something up to use as an exercise as we go through these six steps or lessons. Write that down now.

Gratitude

One of the best ways for us to begin any transformation is to be in this moment and the best way to be in this moment is with gratitude. I want to invite you to pick something that you're grateful for. It can be anything. I pick up my reading glasses whenever I need to look at something. I'm grateful for my glasses. I'm grateful for my eyesight. I'm grateful for you.

I want you to pick something that you're grateful for and, I mean, really feel the gratitude in this moment because gratitude is the single most powerful thing you can do to change your life. I was reading a book earlier, it's actually sitting right here next to me, and it's called *Just Be Glad*. This book is from around 1912. *Just Be Glad*—the title says it all. Throughout the book it keeps saying, "just be glad, just be glad," and everything will change.

The opening line is:

All things respond to the call of rejoicing; all things gather where life is a song. This is the message of the new order, the new life, and the new time. It is the golden text of the great gospel of human sunshine. It is the central truth of that sublime philosophy of existence, which declares that the greatest good is happiness and that heaven is here and now.

I'm inviting you to just be glad. I'm inviting you to find something you're grateful for.

A Pencil—Really?

Let me tell you a quick story of gratitude that I also tell in the movie *The Compass*. A long time ago when I was broke and struggling, I was reading the right books and I was attending the free seminars that kept talking about gratitude. They kept saying be thankful and I thought, *Boy, I'll be thankful when I have something to be thankful for.*

Well as long as I had that skeptical attitude, I wasn't getting anywhere. I remember thinking, "Well maybe I should try this gratitude exercise," and I remember I picked up a pencil. It was a number two pencil, the yellow one with the old lead in it and eraser on top. The one most of us had in school. I certainly did growing up long, long ago.

I looked at the pencil and I said, "Yeah, I'll be grateful for this pencil," and I was flippant about it. I wasn't really into it. I looked at it and I said, "Yeah, with this pencil I can write a suicide note, I can write a grocery list, I can write..." and I started to come up with all the things I could write. I can write a poem. I can write a song. I can write a love letter. I can write a book.

As I started to generate ideas, I shifted inside. I started to truly feel grateful for the pencil. Then I looked at the other side and I saw the eraser and I thought *that's genius*. With an eraser, I can erase the suicide note or I can erase lines of the poem that didn't rhyme or if I wrote a grocery list, I could erase the things I didn't want. Suddenly I looked at the pencil as a miracle!

I thought, *Who invented the pencil?* What an amazing thing a pencil is and it's just a stick! It's a stick with a piece of lead in it that you can write with and a brilliant piece of rubber that you can erase with. That was a turning point in my life because I opened my heart, myself, and everything up. I allowed life to come in and it took the blinders off of me. Instead of being skeptical and unhappy and miserable, I started to feel gratitude for everything and everybody around me.

That's the power of gratitude. It changed my life forever and I'll talk about that a little bit more as we go through the lessons in this book. For right now, I want you to feel gratitude for something. It will bring you into this moment. It'll shift your energy; it'll make you feel good. Just be glad. Remember to just be glad. It'll make you feel better and you'll start to attract more things that match the energy of gratitude.

Your Turn: Gratitude Exercise

Take a moment, close your eyes, and reflect: what are you grateful for? Pick anything—it doesn't matter what—just decide what it is and then feel it. It's very important that you feel it. So feel the gratitude, and allow that to go through your body. If you have to fake it till you make it, that's entirely fine—much like I did with the pencil.

I didn't feel grateful when I first picked up the pencil, but as I pretended to feel grateful, it became sincere gratitude. I felt grateful and it changed my life. It opened me up forever and it'll do the same for you. This is where we begin. We're starting with what you want and we're starting with gratitude—two powerful tools.

The Law of Attraction

Now, many of you are here because of the law of attraction, and that's fine and dandy. Let's talk about the law of attraction. I want to assure you we're going to go beyond the law of attraction. We're going to go into the other laws and we're going to actually transcend the laws so you can work within them and beyond them.

You can transcend the laws. That's an advanced concept and we'll go into that a little bit deeper over the next few chapters, but right now, we want to start with some basics and really take it to a deeper level.

I know you have probably heard of the law of attraction. You may be practicing it or be a fan of it, but the way most people understand the law of attraction is wrong.

Many people have a very superficial understanding of the law of attraction. I want you to understand it deeper. What most people think about the law of attraction is that they're going to get whatever they think about, and at a very superficial level that's true. But you have a lot of thoughts and not all of those thoughts come true. Scientists say you have 60,000 to 80,000 thoughts a day.

Imagine that, 60,000 to 80,000 thoughts a day. Most of the thoughts are the same ones. So you are thinking recycled material all day long, but notice they don't all come true. And you can't help but wonder why. Why don't they all come true?

Many people are looking at the law of attraction but they don't understand what it really is because they're thinking, *Oh, I'll just think it or maybe if I just visualize it, it's going to come into being.* Well you know as well as I, that doesn't always happen. So that raises the question, why not? Is the law of attraction selective? Does it work for everybody else and not work for you?

What is the law of attraction, who does it work for, and how do you make it work? Now that's all part of what we're going to be digging into, in this first lesson in particular, but expanding on through these lessons because, again, I want you to make this work. I care about you. That's why I'm doing this. I'm making time to do this. I want to share everything I've learned in my six-plus decades here.

All the research that I've done, everything that I've been working on, plus my own personal discoveries, all of that, I want to open up and share it with you so you have what really works. I'm an entrepreneur. I'm a results guy. So I don't want to give you airy-fairy things that are just pie-in-the-sky-wispy ideals that don't do anything. I want you to understand how the law of attraction really works.

Belief and the Law of Attraction

The law of attraction is actually working on your beliefs. It's working on your belief system, which for the most part is not what's in your conscious mind. Beliefs are the primary driver of the law of attraction, and not necessarily your conscious beliefs. That's the big mistake everybody keeps making.

They think, if I just sit here and think:

I am now attracting more money
I am now attracting my perfect relationship
I am now attracting my better job
I am now attracting more sales
I am now attracting better health

I am now attracting my ideal home
[Or fill in the blank with whatever you want]

People are thinking it and they might even be visualizing it, but that's not enough. You know why? Because you have a conscious mind and you have an unconscious mind.

The Subconscious Mind and Counterintentions

Some people call your unconscious mind the subconscious mind. Some people call it the non-conscious mind. You know what I'm talking about. You have a conscious mind and you have this deeper iceberg that's below the level of the conscious mind. It's holding your database of beliefs. That's where all of the law of attraction is actually taking place. It's not on the conscious level.

See, consciously, you can be saying to yourself and visualizing, "I'm attracting more money," but if unconsciously you think money is bad or you think money is evil or you think you're bad or you think you're evil or you think money will contaminate you or if you think you don't deserve money or you don't deserve good things or if you think there's a shortage of money or if you think you have to be ruthless to have money or any number of negative things, what do you think is going to happen to your conscious intention? It's going to be crippled. It's going to be destroyed. I call these counterintentions.

In other words, you have intentions, which are the things that you want to attract into your life, but then you can also have counterintentions. The counterintentions are vetoing the intentions, and all of this is based on beliefs. You have a belief system that's operating in your brain and for the most part you're unconscious to it. That's not wrong. That doesn't mean you're dumb. It doesn't mean you're bad. It doesn't mean that you're irresponsible. We all have that. We were programmed from birth with beliefs—not with facts—and we all have a different story about how we were brought up.

Let me ask you this: Were your parents enlightened? Were your parents Mr. and Mrs. Buddha? Most likely they were not. I know that my parents struggled with their own beliefs; beliefs about money. Some of the biggest fights that I heard when I was a kid were with my parents over money. They had their own beliefs about relationships and they had fights about that. I, as a kid, was downloading all of the information assuming that was how the world works. I assumed it was reality. You probably did the same thing.

When you were growing up, you made conclusions. As a child, as an unthinking, unconscious, developing child, you were downloading all this information and making conclusions about the world and how it worked. Those were beliefs. You carried those beliefs into adulthood, like I did. Then at some point, you sat there and you wondered, *How come I can't have the perfect relationship? How come I can't have money? How come I can't have success? How come I can't have... [fill in the blank]?*

It's not your fault; it's your belief system. Other people, not you, created your belief system. Your belief system, most scientists agree, was developed, installed, and almost complete by the time you were seven years old. Imagine that. Most of us are grown up seven-year-olds. I'm seven years old in this body. You're seven years old in your body.

Now, that doesn't mean it has to stay that way, and that's why you're reading this book. We're going to change all that. We're going to remove that. We're going to awaken from that. You're going to change your belief system. I did it too (I'll tell you my little story shortly). So what I'm telling you here is about beliefs, about facts, about intentions, about counterintentions, and then we also want to talk about clearing.

Clearing Out the Old

Clearing is how we're going to remove the counterintentions. Clearing is a process. Throughout this book, we will use a variety of clearing techniques so that you can actually, as the word says, get clear of whatever is going on in your life. When you're trying to attract something and you're not able to do it, it's not your fault, and it's not the law of attraction's fault. You're actually operating the way you were programmed to operate and the law of attraction is actually doing what the law was set up to do. It's attracting to you a match to your unconscious belief system. What we want to clear up are the beliefs that aren't working for you. That's what this is all about.

Now, I also want to tease you a little bit and say we're going to also go beyond this because the law of attraction in many ways is the beginner's law.

Getting clear is a step towards where I really want you to go, which is awakening. Once you awaken, there are no limitations, there are no boundaries; the entire planet becomes yours because at that point you live in the field of all possibilities. There aren't any limits at that point; there are no restrictions. The only limits, the only restrictions, and the only boundaries are in you—they're where your belief system is.

That's why all of this is so important, and that's why most of the self-help programs that are out there don't work. They don't work because they're missing this secret. This is *the missing secret*.

You've got to understand that when people tell you, "Just do this or just believe that or just visualize this or just feel this or just think this or just write affirmations," or just do whatever, people are giving you an incomplete recipe. They're still working on the conscious level of beliefs. If you have an intention and you've had one for a while and you've not been able to attract it or achieve it, no doubt it's because of your unconscious beliefs, your counterintentions. The missing secret is you must get clear of the counterintentions so you can have your intentions come into your life.

The Secret: It's Only the Beginning

Now, you probably saw the movie *The Secret*. If you haven't seen the movie *The Secret*, I encourage you to see it because it's a great movie. It's at www.thesecret.tv. It's probably on Netflix and Amazon and everywhere else. Now, the movie is wonderful and it's all about the law of attraction. That movie introduced the law of attraction to the world and it took the world by storm. It is still traveling the planet. The movie came out ten years ago and it's still moving, still selling.

There's also a book called *The Secret* that's based on the movie. I'm glad that I'm in both the book and the movie—I'm very proud of it. I would encourage you to see the movie or read the book whether I was in it or not, but there is a problem with it and that's why there are so many skeptics. That's why there are so many critics who make fun of *The Secret* or make fun of the law of attraction. The movie introduced the idea of the law of attraction. It introduced the idea and that's all it was supposed to do, but everybody assumed that because of what they saw in the movie, that's how the law of attraction worked. That's an incomplete story.

The law of attraction works deeper than what the movie revealed. People watched the movie and they thought, *Oh, well, all I have to do is sit in a chair and close my eyes and visualize a bike and the doorbell will ring and my uncle will be there with a bike.* Or they say, "All I have to do is visualize, oh, my perfect house, mmm, I can feel being in it. Then I go down the street and I discover my perfect house."

The movie led you to believe that it was so simple that it was almost like your life could be a Walt Disney movie. I am not saying your life can't be like that. Those kinds of things can happen, but only once you use the missing secret. Only once you get clear of the counterintentions, the counter beliefs, and the old programming. Then you might sit in a chair and visualize the bike. Then the doorbell will ring and a bike will be there because there won't be any interference in you to keep that kind of a miracle from taking place.

The vast majority of people watched the movie and made the erroneous assumption that that's all they had to do. Think it, visualize it, and it shows up. Again, if you don't have any blocks, and you don't have any counterintentions, that's what may happen. But most of us have blocks; most of us have counterintentions.

My Story

I don't know if you know my story, but it's probably worth mentioning here that I haven't always been the author that you see before you or the musician that I am now or a guy in a movie as I am now. I don't know if you know this, but I was homeless at one point, back in the 1970s. I used to avoid talking about this because it was embarrassing and it was traumatizing and it was psychologically damaging. I was embarrassed to share it. It was a personal, private experience and I didn't think anybody needed to know about it, but over time, as I became more well known and my books became published and my name got out there more, people would ask me about my early story. Then I would start to tell it and they would be inspired.

Then I thought, *Well maybe that's why I need to tell it.* People think if Joe can leave homelessness and become this best selling author who lives the lifestyle of the rich and famous and gets to do wonderful books like this, then maybe their lives can change too. Yes, your life can change too; mine did.

I was homeless in Dallas, Texas, in the late 1970s, and then I moved to Houston. I don't know how I got there (bus, hitchhiked, I don't actually remember), but I was in poverty for ten years. I was married during that time and it was really rough for both of us. I remember being depressed. I remember even being suicidal. I remember being so unhappy I would cry. I managed to get a job that I hated and I would drive to work crying behind the wheel of the car. I'd drive home crying behind the wheel of the car. I was that unhappy.

I had my goal. I wanted to be an author. So you see, I had my intention. It was a noble intention. I wasn't drinking. I wasn't into drugs. I wasn't doing any of the addictive behaviors that a lot of people say got them into homelessness or poverty. I was trying my best. I had a noble goal. I wanted to make a difference in the planet. I felt like it was my calling to be an author, but why wasn't it happening? Why was I struggling?

I was so broke—I get emotional even thinking about it, just sharing it with you—I remember my wife was making some spaghetti one night; great comfort food for an Italian like me, right? She dropped the jar of tomato sauce and it broke on the floor and shattered and I didn't have the $2.17 to go buy another jar. It was kind of the symbol of my life; when the car would break down, it was a catastrophe because I didn't have the money to fix it.

We lived in this little room with the toilet in the same room as the TV and our fold out bed, and it cost $200 a month. I struggled to pay it. I know what it's like to struggle. I know what it's like to be homeless. I also know what it's like to awaken and get past that. So everybody asks me all the time, "How did you get past that? How did you awaken? How did you get out of homelessness? How did you get out of poverty? What did you do?"

The Turn-Around

I'm going to tell you what I did. I did everything. I read all the books. I listened to the audios. I lived in the public library. I've always been a book addict. I've got books all around me. I now have two offices worth of books, and libraries, and I've also given away many books. I love books: reading them, writing them—I'm addicted to books. I'm a bookaholic.

I lived in the public library virtually, literally, when I was in Dallas, Texas, because that's where I escaped the elements. I escaped the heat. I found comfort and air conditioning and water in the bathroom at the public library in Dallas.

I read books like *Just Be Glad, How to Turn Your Desires and Ideals into Reality*, and *The Science of Getting Rich* from the early 1900s. I have original editions of all these books now. I even have a book by William Walker Atkinson who was the one who invented the term "law of attraction" in the early 1900s. These books are part of my collection. But back then, I was reading these books while I was at the library, and I was learning about the law of attraction.

As you can tell, I was learning about all of this while I was homeless, and I didn't have courses and programs like we have now. You're so lucky to invest in books like this, and with technology today, you can be in your home, I can be in my home, and we can meet and dance together, electronically.

I'm grateful for the books. I read all of these books from the 1900s during the 1970s, and these books were changing my life because they were teaching me all these things. *Attaining Your Desires* by Genevieve

Behrend was a book that so influenced me that I later republished it. That's how far I came in my career by learning how the law of attraction really works.

So what was the big *aha* for me? I'm in the library in Dallas. I am homeless. I don't have a home. People said, "What kind of car did you live in?" I didn't have a car. A car would have been nice, but I didn't have a car. I was literally homeless.

So I'm in a public library, and I'm reading these books. I'm learning about the law of attraction and I'm thinking to myself, *How do I make this work?* Because, back then, I didn't have a coach. I didn't have anybody to talk to. I was single at that point. I was totally by myself. I didn't have the Internet. The Internet wasn't even invented yet; nor was a Mac computer. I didn't have any of this stuff that you have now.

There I am wrestling with these materials by myself, really being forced to look in the mirror. Then I realized, with quite a shock, that I was basing my life on a belief. Get this, I was basing my life on a belief, *a belief I wasn't conscious of.* I had a driving belief that was organizing everything I was attracting in my life and I didn't even know what it was.

Through all these books, through self-reflection, through looking in the mirror at myself, and being ruthlessly honest, I realized that I had admired these dramatic authors who had these flamboyant, dangerous, unhappy lives like Jack London. He wrote *The Call of the Wild* and *Martin Eden* and *White Fang* and *The Sea*

Wolf and fifty other books. I also followed Ernest Hemingway who wrote *The Old Man and the Sea* and a bunch of other books.

I was modeling my life unconsciously on them. I thought that I had to have an unhappy, dramatic, melodramatic life in order to be a famous author too. Now, I hope you grasp what an awakening this was for me because I suddenly realized that everything in my life was because of me; everything in my life was being attracted to me. The law of attraction was alive and well and it was working, but it was working on my unconscious belief at that time and my unconscious belief said I had to suffer to be an author.

All the years I suffered. All the stuff I went through. All the suicidal, melancholy, broke, desperate unhappy days, and ten years worth of them because of that thought. So when I changed that thought, when I got clear of that thought and I started to ask myself what other beliefs might I have, I started to realize that I could choose it.

In other words, I began to think to myself, *Well, if there're authors out there who are unhappy and productive, but suicidal and dramatic, much like Jack London and Ernest Hemingway, then there must be authors out there who are happy, who are prolific, who are productive, who are actually making a difference and making money and helping people, and doing it while being in health and prosperity.* I thought, *Let me find those authors and model them.* When I started to think like them, then my life changed.

So that's what happened to me. It still was a slow effort because I still had to change all the other beliefs in me and change them by myself. In other words, I was working on me by myself—just me operating on me. That's a little bit like trying to play chess with yourself. You know all of your next moves, so you can't outsmart yourself, and that's what I was trying to do—outsmart my own belief system.

That's tough to do. You can do it, but it's tough to do. That's why I'm so grateful that you're reading this book. By working through this material, together, we're going to unravel and erase the negative limiting beliefs—the ones that aren't serving you. You can certainly keep the beliefs that are serving you, but you want to release the beliefs that aren't serving you. That'll free you so you can have, do, or be whatever you want.

Common Questions

I want to take a few moments, here, and at each step that follows, to share common questions that arise as I cover this material with others. It is my hope that my answers to these questions will help you too. I encourage you to read through the answers, even if you don't initially think the question pertains to you. You might be amazed at how much you learn that you can apply in your own life.

Are there certain categories of base beliefs that we need to work on?

There definitely are. I wrote a book called *Attract Money Now*, which you can have free. (You can go to attractmoneynow.com and just download it.) In that book, I talk about base beliefs. Some of the base beliefs are things like *I'm not lovable, I don't deserve success, or I'm not good enough.*

Now, those three beliefs are the foundation beliefs to a whole lot of other problems. Those three beliefs are the root to a bunch of other problems in life. So, you can imagine if somebody is trying to attract their ideal relationship and they think unconsciously *I'm not lovable* or *I am not deserving of success* or *I'm not good enough*—if they have any variation of those beliefs, it's going to be difficult for them to actually attract what they want into their life.

So, first, become aware of the beliefs. You're going to find out how powerful awareness alone is. When you find out what a belief is, suddenly you know, "Oh, that's been operating in my brain," and you can ask yourself, "Do I want to keep this or not?" Then at that point you can decide and just let it go or you can say, "Yes, I'm good enough." Then it's gone.

You may need to do more than that. I admit that during my homeless years, during my poverty years, I had to go into the bathroom and look in the mirror and actually look at myself and begin to love myself. I'd have to look in the mirror and say, "Okay, people say you have beautiful brown eyes. Yeah, I guess I do. I do like my eyes, I do love my eyes," and I would start there. I'd look at my eyes.

Then I'd look at something else with me. People always told me, "You have great dimples." Then I would look at my dimples and go, "Oh, those must be okay." Begin somewhere. Much like with the exercise with the pencil, when I picked it up, I was skeptical and I didn't have any gratitude for the pencil, but as I began the process, I started to develop gratitude for it.

What we're doing here is beginning to love ourselves again when we may not have had it before. You can start now. That is a primary belief and that's a great question to address.

How do we ensure that we know the lessons that we have learned from the beliefs so we can let them go?

This question typically comes from somebody who has read one of my books; because in my book *The Attractor Factor*, I said when you get the lesson, you no longer need the experience.

Now, this is a little deep, but what we're talking about here is the lesson is actually the belief that caused the experience. Another way to look at this is the meaning you give an event is actually the belief that attracted the event. ***The meaning you give an event is***

actually the belief that attracted the event. In other words, your beliefs are creating your reality in every way, shape, or form, but you don't even know what the beliefs are, so you need to discover them.

> *"The meaning you give an event is actually the belief that attracted the event."*

One way to do that is to pay attention to how you tell your story about your beliefs. This will unravel the core operating belief in your unconscious so you can release it, and then you're free to have, do, or be whatever it is that you were wanting to attract or achieve. So now you want to pay attention to the stories, and a good way to do this is to imagine you're having lunch with somebody and you're talking about the experience of not making enough money.

Notice how you describe it. You might say something like, "Well darn it, I'm still not making enough money at work. I'm working my butt off, but I'm not making the money. I think it's all stacked up against me; it's never going to work out." Stop there. That line *I think it's all stacked up against me; it's never going to work out*, is a belief. You said it as a summary giving meaning to the story, but what really was going on is that you were revealing the operating belief and didn't know it.

Since the time we will spend together with this book is all about awakening, what I want you to realize is that the more you pay attention to how you speak and the more you pay attention to how you think, the more you'll unravel the core beliefs, and then you'll get the lessons. Once you know what the belief is, you basically have the lesson and the belief leaves.

How do you know when the belief has left for good? When that experience doesn't happen anymore. The lack, the problem, the limitation, the scarcity, it doesn't happen anymore. It's over. It's gone. In fact, you'll probably even find it difficult to remember it. When you really complete a belief, you will be free of it. You will have gotten the lesson.

How do I deal with other people's projections onto me?

That's an interesting question, too, because we want to go deeper than what most people are thinking about other people. As we go through this material, you're going to find out that everything in your life is the projection from within you. Now, in future chapters, we're going to go into this a little bit more deeply, and you'll understand that more.

Again, because we're just starting out on this journey together, a lot of the things I'm sharing with you might be a little confusing. Some things might be a little hard to understand or grasp or make real in your life because they are deeper concepts than most people know about. They're deeper than what most other books talk about.

Again, I really want to be of the most help to you, so I have to be truly honest with you and tell you this is how the world works.

This is what I've discovered from everything from my homeless years to my poverty years to my struggle to success to going beyond all comprehension and the success that I have today. Everything that I've learned, everything that I've done, all the material I've studied, all of the exercises, the meditations I've worked on, all the awakenings I've had to lead to the big awakening in my own life has lead me to understand that the world works in ways that most of us don't comprehend.

One of the ways it works is that life is a mirror and it's reflecting to you what you believe. Let's look at other people. If there are other people in your life and they're saying things about you or to you or they're being negative or they're being critical, it's not about them. It's not about them. They are actually demonstrating what you believe unconsciously inside yourself and I'm being very gentle as I say this because this is huge.

This is a huge moment for an awakening. Part of the miracle can take place right now when you realize that you are responsible for all of it, for everything. This does not mean that you are guilty or you are bad or you are negative or you are unawake or anything. It doesn't mean anything negative at all. To awaken is to realize that you are responsible for everything because you're attracting everything.

There are no exceptions to the law of attraction. It's like saying there're exceptions to gravity. If I drop my glasses here, they're going to fall because of gravity, and if I do everything that we've been taught to do, the law of attraction is going to bring me what I believe unconsciously in my life. It's just going to be automatic. It's going to be automatic and even mechanical and it's going to be neutral.

It's not going to judge. It's just going to bring to you a match to your beliefs. So if there is somebody in your life that is actually being negative and so forth, what you have to reflect on is, "Are they voicing something I secretly believe too?" That's cause for a deep awakening. That is cause for some deep soul-searching. That is cause for you to really look within.

You've invested in this material because you want miracles. You are to expect miracles; you want miracles, and that's why you're reading this book. So I want you to take on what I'm talking about and own it; really befriend it, really meditate on it, and find out just how true it is for you because there's great freedom that comes from this insight. When you realize it's not about other people, but that actually the other people are reflecting what's in you, then you realize the place to change is in you. When you change you, son of a gun, they will either change or they will leave or they will say whatever they say but it won't bother you anymore because your buttons inside you will be gone. Think about that. That's a massive insight.

How quickly can I expect results?

You're already getting results. It's really important to know that we're all instant manifestors.

We are instant manifestors. Right now, we are manifesting this moment. Now on my Facebook fan page, which you might want to visit at some point, I'm always posting little thought-provoking triggers. One day, I posted there the whole idea that your thoughts that you're thinking right now will generally come to be in three days. Think about that. The thoughts you're thinking right now, especially the ones you're thinking with emotion—with feeling—will tend to come about in three days.

Now, why don't they always come about? Because we change our mind, we take off the fuel, the emotion, or the fire that motivates them. If you start coming from the place of choosing something you want with a thought, a thought expresses what you want. You choose something you want and then you fuel it with emotion.

For example, imagine how you would love having a new car or love having a relationship. So, you have the emotion and you have the thought that will tend to come about in three days unless you have a counter thought. The way to find those is to choose something. You choose, "I want $5,000 in unexpected income by next Friday." Then you fuel it with emotion. "Oh, it'll be so exciting to have $5,000 in unexpected income. It'll be joyful. I can celebrate. I can pay bills. I can take my spouse out to eat. I can...[do whatever it is for you that feels good]!"

So, you have all the emotion coming up. Your vibration is coming up and your thought has laser focus going right to what you want. All of those are working together, and then you notice what shows up. Do you have counter thoughts? Do you have thoughts that say, "Yeah, but how is this going to happen?" We want to get rid of the how thought. It doesn't matter how. What matters is what: what do you want to have, do, or be?

More people get tripped up by focusing on how, than about anything else because they'll say something like, "Well I want to open my own business, but I don't know how." We learn how to do everything, so we don't need to know how to get the $5,000 in unexpected income; we just need to know we want it and we feel good thinking about it. Then we take inspired action whenever we have the feeling towards it.

If we get a nudge to attend a class or buy a book or call somebody or go on Google and get some information, then follow through with the inspired nudge or with the intuition that's propelling you forward.

We're already instant manifestors. You manifested this moment. You manifested this moment by what you already thought and what you already felt and what you already did. These are clues on how to manifest whatever you want.

I wrote a book called *Instant Manifestation* and the whole idea was that we're already manifesting. We just don't think we are because we're thinking that we're pushing everything off in the distance and we're forgetting that the real miracle is right now. The real miracle is here now. We can focus on the real miracle being here now, and then out of this now, have the thought and feel-good emotion for what we want. Then take inspired action when we get inspired to do something and intuition kicks in. Then we'll make all the next moments miracles as well.

How do I discover my negative beliefs?

Well they're not really hiding. All you have to do is think, and be aware of your thinking, and you will find them. As I mentioned earlier, we have 60,000 to 80,000 thoughts a day. Most of them are the same thoughts and most of them are negative.

When you pay attention to your thoughts, you find out that most of it is criticizing yourself. This goes back to some of those fundamental beliefs about not feeling good enough, not feeling lovable, not feeling like you have enough or are resourceful in any way, shape, or form, or simply putting yourself down. Those are negative beliefs. So what I'm asking you to do, especially in this first lesson, is become aware of your thinking.

In fact, I'm not sure how to really stress how important this is because in many ways, we have six lessons together in this book, and this first one is kind of like a wake up call. It's kind of like the beginning of an awakening or it's the first of six awakenings if you want to put it that way. I want you to become very clear of your thoughts. As you're becoming clear of your thoughts, don't buy into them.

In other words, pretend your thoughts are like you're listening to the radio. The radio is playing, but you're not the radio. You're detached from the radio and you're just hearing the radio. So you're separate from the radio. I want you to be separate from your thoughts. As you're thinking, right now you're thinking, you're reading my words and you've got thoughts going on. As you're thinking, even right now, what are your thoughts tending to be like?

You might even write them down because when you see them on paper, you're able to separate yourself and be a little bit more objective and realize that those thoughts aren't you. Those thoughts are revealing a basic belief system. They will reveal any negative beliefs, they'll also reveal positive beliefs, but the nature of the mind is to always send thoughts up. It seems like that's its job. It's going to send thoughts.

Now, over these six lessons together, your thoughts will become more and more positive and they'll get to the point where almost all the thoughts that bubble up are going to be positive, supportive, nurturing, and objective thoughts. The negative thoughts, the critical thoughts, the downer thoughts will start to leave. This is really another miracle waiting for you because the more you pay attention to your thoughts, no matter what they are, and you realize that you are not your thoughts, the more freedom you have.

You have great freedom and you're one step closer to enlightenment. You're one step closer to awakening. You're one step closer to living the miracle. At that point you don't just expect miracles, you actually live the miracles and that's where I really want you to get. I want you to get to the point where you live the miracle. I want you to look around and have moment-by-moment awe and wonder at the miraculous life that we're sharing together.

That's where I want you to be. If you, just today, started to focus on "Let's pay attention to my thoughts, let me write down my predominant thoughts," you'll probably be shocked to find that most of the thoughts are about worry, they're about fear, they're about criticism, and they're about doubt. Those are your thoughts, but you are not your thoughts. You're separate from the thoughts. The thoughts are bubbling up from a belief system and we're going to change the belief system.

In fact, this moment is beginning to change because a lot of what we're doing here—the information and the sharing—is causing an awakening within you. You should also know that I'm trained as an energy healer in Qigong, Reiki, and a bunch of other modalities, and as I'm sharing these words with you, I'm sending energy to you. We are all one on a very deep level. So, when I send energy to you to help clear you and enlighten you and raise your vibration, it's reaching you because we're all one.

There's no real separation in the world. Deep underneath everything, underneath the flesh and bones and the thoughts and the bodies and the feelings and everything else, the thinking mechanism that's going on, we're one. This will make more sense to you as we go through this book. So don't worry about the negative thoughts. Don't worry at all. In fact, let's go back and just be glad.

Just be glad and focus on gratitude. Focus on sincerity. Focus on what you want with love. At the same time, be aware of the thoughts that come up. Write them down, but remind yourself you are not those thoughts. You are separate from those thoughts.

If it feels like somebody is holding you back, is it them holding you back or is it you?

The advanced concept is—it's you. That's the advanced concept. Again, you've invested in working with this material because you want a transformation. If you want the true transformation then you have to grasp these deeper concepts. It's not about the other person. Nobody is holding you back. I know it feels like they are. That's the illusion that's around us.

We live in a movie theatre. We live in a mirage. What I mean is the movie projector is actually in your head. The movie projector is in your skull and shooting out through your eyes. You're seeing the movie of life but that movie is being written and scripted and propelled and acted out in our head, in the back of your own head. So all the work needs to be done there.

Now, in future lessons I'm going to take this apart for you. In one lesson farther along in the book I'm going to teach you a technique that is so profound and so powerful and so miraculous in changing what appears to be other people, but you're changing yourself in the simplest way.

It's a simple technique but I'll tell you the whole story then and I'll walk you through the whole exercise. It's very easy. I do it all the time. In fact, I'm doing it right now. I'm doing that technique for you within myself. I do it automatically because I've been doing this one technique for over ten years. This one technique will help you resolve what appear to be issues with the other people in your life, but it will do it by changing the projector in you.

Maybe another way to look at this is like a spiritual teacher of mine who says, "Have you ever noticed that when there's a problem, you are always there?" Have you ever noticed when you have an issue with another person, you are there? It isn't the other person—it's you. The button that you're feeling, whether you call it "the holding back button" or something else, isn't in them, it's in you.

So, when you release that button, they won't be there anymore. They'll either move on, they'll stop doing whatever you perceive that they're doing, or it won't matter anymore. It'll be over with, it'll be removed, it'll vanish, or it'll be cleared. So it isn't about the other people, it is about you. Again, I know that is so difficult to hear.

When I was homeless, if somebody walked up to me and said, "Hey, it's your fault that you're homeless." Or they said that, "Hey, the whole world is a projection coming out of your head so you're homeless because of yourself," I probably would have socked them. I wasn't in a place to accept that kind of wisdom, because it wasn't wisdom then. Then, I was in the survival. Then, I was in the struggle. It's important to realize that that's how your mind is geared.

Your mind is geared to keep you alive so it's on alert to look for threats to your environment. That's the primary job of your brain. And because it's trying to keep you safe, it is looking around and it's finding all the danger and warning signs that are around you, whether it's from other people or the economy or wherever it happens to be.

We want to get beyond all of that. You're going to have to elevate yourself out of that earth-level drama and together we're going to do it. Now, don't expect all of this to happen overnight. It might happen tonight between what I'm doing for you and what you're already getting from this and the exercises you do. It might all happen really quickly, but this is designed to happen over the course of this book, beginning today.

How does a spouse's belief affect my outcome?

It's the same thing. It's not your spouse. It's you. Your spouse is responding to you on an unconscious level. Now, this is a big insight into how relationships work. I know it feels like you're walking around saying, "Hey, I'm going to achieve these miracles. I'm reading *The Miracle* with Joe Vitale," and the spouse says something negative or the spouse says, "Oh, that's not going to help." Or the spouse says, "Oh I heard about that guy; he's not that great." There're all kinds of things that people can say.

Remember, it's not about them. Stop and think: if that bothers you, if what the spouse says bothers you, it's because you have a button in you that is agreeing with them.

An unconscious part of you is aligning with what they're saying—not a conscious part. Remember, it's the unconscious that is the database of all the beliefs. The unconscious mind is bigger and more powerful and older than the conscious mind. The conscious mind is this tiny little pipsqueak up in your head.

Scientists say that the conscious mind sees about seven bits of information—seven—in any moment. Just seven. The unconscious mind sees about twelve million bits of information in any one moment. So consciously we think we're directing our lives and we're running the ship. We are not. The unconscious mind is. So our beliefs are in the unconscious mind, our data is in the unconscious mind, our programs are in the unconscious mind, and our mindset, our paradigm is all there.

When you walk into the living room, your spouse isn't just responding to what you say, he or she is responding to your database in your unconscious. They're picking up on signals that you're not even aware that you're sending. So what they're doing is a gift. They're reflecting back to you your own beliefs.

Now, I'm the first to say you have to have support. I am not dismissing that at all. I am a great believer in having support. I just have to be of the most service to you and make sure you understand that a spouse is a mirror and somebody that close in a relationship is going to reflect more accurately some of your deeply held beliefs. So if the spouse says something negative or limiting, you really have to ask yourself, "Do I believe on some level what they're saying?" and then begin the process of getting clear.

Now, remember just being aware of these things is going to be a great step in getting clear. Then going through the different exercises I'll be giving you in the pages ahead will help you dissolve these things almost by magic, almost instantly; but right now we're just awakening. We're becoming aware of our thoughts. We're becoming aware of our intentions. We're becoming aware of our gratitude. We're becoming aware of processes we can use to help us to just be glad.

How do I get through the fear of living a successful life?

This is another great question. The fear of living a successful life is very akin to why people procrastinate. There are really three reasons why people procrastinate, but let's look at the first two. There's the fear of failure and there's the fear of success.

The first is the fear of failure. The fear of failure is what most people identify with first, though it's not as powerful as the fear of success. With the fear of failure, everybody feels like they'll be ashamed that they'll be scarred. Like there will be a Scarlet Letter on them of some sort.

The truth of the matter is that doesn't happen at all. I remember I interviewed a billionaire a decade ago (a billionaire with a B), and he said that he had failed many times and he learned something profound from failure.

I said, "Well, what was that?"

He said, "Nothing bad happens." He said, "The world forgets and the world forgives. You just go on. In fact, I look at failure as feedback."

If I try something and it doesn't work, it doesn't mean it failed, it means that I get information to help me tweak, fine tune, spin, put on a new angle, create a different product, or whatever it happens to be. It's just simply feedback. So we can take away the fear of failure because there is no such thing. Nobody really cares. Life goes on and you use what other people call failure as feedback.

Well, what about the fear of success (which is akin to the primary question)? That's also aligning itself with the idea that you want to be liked and you want to be loved. The fear of success deals with things like "What will my family think, what will my friends think, will people be jealous, will people try to misuse me, will I become a bad person, will I become a different person, will success taint me, or will success be bad?" As you can see, these are all very negative-oriented downer beliefs.

What I learned about success is it's all good. It's all good. I remember at one point in my career I was struggling but doing better. The Internet had come along, I had a book or two published, I was making more money, and I realized that there seemed to be a ceiling to how much money I was making. I wondered why there was a ceiling there. There shouldn't be a ceiling at all. Why do I keep making that much money and I stop? Why can't I make more?

Then I started to analyze it. This is how you find your beliefs—you start asking questions. I asked myself why I was not allowing more money to come into my life. There's nobody restricting me from having more money. A lot of the money was coming from the Internet. There's no watchdog on the Internet saying you can't have more money.

So it must be me. I thought *why wouldn't I want more money? Why am I hitting this ceiling and not going any higher?* Then I realized I didn't want to be more successful than my father. That had been a hidden belief. That had been an unconscious counterintention. That had been a belief operating like a pseudo fact to keep me from my own good.

So I asked myself "Is that true?" which is another thing you can do with beliefs. You find what the belief is and then you ask, "Is it true?" I asked myself, "Is it true?" Would my father be embarrassed or be hurt or feel like a failure if I was more successful? I immediately knew the answer was no. He'd be happy for me. He wants the best for me. When I realized that, the ceiling left. There is no ceiling now because it was an invisible ceiling. It was a wealth set point based on a subconscious, unconscious, non-conscious desire not to be successful.

So that's what I invite you to do. Look at why you might not want to have a successful life. Then whatever questions or answers come up, write them down, look at them, and ask, "Are these true?" Look at the answers and ask, "Is this true?" "Do I not want to be successful because I think I'll be a bad person? Is that true?" Most likely you'll say no. You're a good person now. You're not going to be a bad person because you're successful, so it's a belief.

As I mentioned earlier, we have to know the difference between beliefs and facts. If somebody says, "I don't like yellow shirts," that's their belief. If somebody says, "I only wear yellow shirts," it's probably a fact unless we catch them one day not wearing one.

So, we want to be aware of the difference between beliefs and facts. We want to be aware of what we're thinking, what we're sharing, and what we're doing. Don't be afraid of success. Success is good. We'll talk about more about that as we move through the six steps, but you have to realize that the more successful you are, the happier you are, the healthier you are, and, in addition, you can help more people.

I can help my family. I can help friends. I have helped complete strangers. I have contributed to causes I believe in. I started a movement to end homelessness because I was successful enough to do it. You can make a difference in your life and other people's lives when you realize success is good and you are good.

―――

Attraction Takes Action

I mentioned procrastination earlier and I said there were three reasons why people didn't take action. One is the fear of success. We talked about it: don't be afraid to be successful. Another is a fear of failure: there is no such thing as failure, its just feedback; take the information that comes, twist it, and move forward. Then the third reason people don't take action is because they're overwhelmed. A lot of people delay in taking action because the project they want is too big. They don't know where to start.

What I learned to do is break everything down into manageable baby steps: one or two steps that you begin now. Now, this is really important—don't dismiss this. What I'm saying is you may have a giant goal to open some sort of business. You want to open a restaurant. You want to write a book. You want to start a Fortune 500 business. That might seem overwhelming. It might seem colossal, and it might seem suffocating to you because it's so big.

Leave it as the goal and then just ask yourself one question, "What's the first thing I can do right now?" Maybe it is just simply getting the website for whatever the business is. Maybe it is opening up a document file and beginning to write the first sentence of the book. You take the baby step first. Here's what happens, here's the big secret: When you take the baby step, the next step becomes apparent. When you take that step, the next step after it becomes apparent.

By taking these baby steps, you can walk across the United States; you can do anything, by doing one little step at a time.

The other example might be that if you were driving your car late at night and it's dark, you'll have to turn the headlights on. You can only see a hundred yards or so ahead of you, but you can drive across the United States while only seeing a hundred yards in front of you. As you drive that hundred yards, the next hundred yards becomes visible. As you drive that hundred yards, the next hundred yards becomes visible. By doing that, you can drive all the way across the country. It's the same thing with anything that you want to create.

So look at why you aren't taking action right now. Again, it could have been the fear of success. We've already looked at that. Success is good, and success is good for you. You are a good person, you are a loving person, and you deserve it.

We looked at the fear of failure. There is no such thing. It's feedback, and whatever it is, if it didn't work out the way you wanted, look at how it did work out, because often life or the universe itself is directing us where it wants us to go. We say, "I want to go here," and as you start moving there, life bumps you over a little bit and says, "No, you should be going over here," and as you do that, you actually get things done. You actually manifest miracles because you pay attention to the signs and clues.

One Creation at a Time

I also want to point out that this is how I live my life. I don't know if you know this, but I've written fifty books. I am also a musician and I have fifteen albums out—fifteen albums in about four years. That astonishes even me.

I have more digital products, e-books, and downloadable resources than I can even remember—a hundred or two hundred of them, I don't even know. I have about seventy e-books that have not been released yet. I am prolific; I am productive, but if I had to sit down back when I was homeless and in poverty and say, "Joe, you've got to write fifty books and you have to record fifteen albums. You've got to write seventy e-books that won't be released for a while and you've got to come up with a Miracle's Coaching® course and you've got to come up with DVDs and this, that, and the other," I probably would have died in the ditch.

It was too much; it was overwhelming. But instead, I just did the very first thing. I wrote my first book. It was published in 1984. That's what I did first. From there, you do whatever is next. In my case, all these decades later, I now have a pretty big bibliography. I've written a lot, created a lot, and I'm still doing it. This is all possible for you.

This is Your Time

Please understand that this is your moment because you've already invested in yourself. You've taken that first step. We're going to be going deep. I'm going to be giving you more processes and more meditations. I'm going to be holding your hands and we're going to really unravel how the world works, so you can have, do, and be whatever you want. But you have to begin now by loving yourself and knowing you deserve it and knowing you are good enough. You've already proven it by investing in you.

You are worth it. If need be, go look in the mirror and start telling yourself "I love you, I appreciate you." You deserve all good things. It all begins there.

The Path Ahead

We do have five more of these steps to take, but I really want to get you even more excited because in the next step I'm going to tell you how the mind works. I'm going to show you how to program your mind for success. I'm going to show you how to program your mind with a three-step formula that is a breeze to do so you can have, do, or be virtually anything.

You see, right now your brain is already programmed, but as I said, it's programmed for lack and limitation and it's not your fault. It came from people who weren't enlightened and who were coming from lack and limitation in their own brains. They lived that life, and they taught you that, but you're breaking free and you are leaving it.

This is the defining moment. This is the defining process. This is where everything transforms forever. I'm really excited about your next lesson because this is where you actually get to manifest things and get almost instant results. You're going to intend something and then you're going to wire your brain using only these three steps. Again, they're very easy; they'll help you get what you're asking for very quickly. You'll astonish yourself it'll be so quick.

I am Grateful for You

Again, I am very grateful that you are here and I want to remind you of the power of gratitude. I talked about gratitude earlier when I told you the story of the pencil. I want you to realize that I'm grateful for you. I love you, I believe in you, I care about you, and I'm going to do my best to help you in these next five steps, the six steps total, as you read this book.

I am proud of you for stepping forward. I'm proud of you for being here now and I want you to meditate on a new mantra. I want you to have this new slogan—make a bumper sticker out of it if you like—but just start saying to yourself, "Expect miracles, expect miracles, expect miracles." Godspeed to you and I will see you in the next step. Thank you.

STEP TWO

The RAS Intention

There is a wide difference between thinking **of** *what you want in this world and thinking* **from** *what you want.*
—Neville Goddard

Welcome to step two of *The Miracle*. I hope you had a fantastic time since taking the first step. I want to applaud you. I literally want to applaud you for doing this. I want to applaud you because you're doing something fantastic for yourself. You're transforming your life.

You already went through the first lesson, which had a lot of processes and information in it. I shared quite a bit about me so you knew who you were learning from, I had an assignment for you, and, of course, you've had time to practice what you've been learning here. So I'm proud of you and I want to applaud you. I think you should also applaud yourself.

I think you should probably get an app like that. Seriously. It's called *Instant Applause*. There's another one called *Rent-A-Crowd*. They're either free or a dollar, but there's nothing wrong with applauding yourself just to say you're doing it and you're doing something good for yourself. This helps you feel better about yourself. This helps you love yourself. This helps you approve of yourself.

This is all for your highest good. It's all to build up that inner core so you can have, do, or be anything. It is designed to raise your energy so you can actually go out there and accomplish, by God, miracles, and that's what this is all about. *To expect miracles*. That's the mantra I left you with and I hope that you're starting to use it because in the first lesson, I said it's all about expecting miracles and expecting miracles is a mindset. It's a paradigm shift. It's a belief.

Most people have those bumper stickers that say, expect crap to happen, but what we want is to *expect miracles*. The more you move into that mindset, that belief, that way of living, that way of being from the inside out, the more it becomes your reality. So I'm proud of you. I welcome you back. We're going to go on here with the next lesson.

The RAS Intention

What we're talking about in this session is what I'm calling "The RAS Intention." This is a very exciting intention here and it's a very exciting lesson because this is where you really get results. You're setting the stage to program your mind to work with the universe so that you can attract whatever it is that you're after and we want to do something big here. We want to do something notable.

I want you to go out there and attract something you really want and then brag about it. Brag about it to me, tell all your family and friends, tell people on Facebook, on Twitter, and everywhere else about how you're succeeding.

There's an audio of a woman who won $40 million dollars in the lottery using the principles I'm teaching. Now stop and imagine, this woman won $40 million dollars and she says openly in her conversation about how she did it. She read Joe Vitale's books, she applied what I'm teaching, and she did a few other things but she won $40 million dollars.

Now, I'm not encouraging you to play the lottery. I'm not encouraging you to gamble. I'm not encouraging you to even buy a lotto ticket. That's not what it's about. What it's about is having, doing, and being what you truly want, and accomplishing it when you follow the principles I'm teaching. So there's evidence all around that this is going to work for you.

It is probably already working for you and you may not even be aware of it because things are happening a little bit more smoothly for you. So what we're talking about in this second lesson, which is a really juicy one, is how your mind works. It is what I call The RAS Intention.

We're going to go over it as much as we can here, but I want to begin with what is likely to be on your mind. We will start with a few common questions from those at this stage in the process.

―――

Common Questions

I am very focused on the how. The how has a particularly strong pull because it has worked really well for me. Why can't I focus on the how if it works? Do you have suggestions on how to move out of the how and focus more on the what?

What I discussed in the first step is the idea that you don't want to get hung up on the how.

The way the law of attraction works, and the way all the advance laws and principles we'll be talking about over these next lessons work, is that they're guiding principles. You don't want to violate them by thinking you can outsmart them. What most people do is think, *Oh, I know how to accomplish my goal.* It doesn't matter what your goal is—to get a new car, a house, a relationship, better health, a new job, or spiritual enlightenment—the first thing that happens is your mind will tell you how to accomplish it.

Here's the big insight: your mind doesn't know all the different ways to accomplish something. Your mind thinks it does, but your mind, which is basically your ego, is basing its ideas on what's been done in the past. This is crucial. Your mind is telling you, "Here's the way to do it," and it's telling you that based on what it read, what it experienced, or what it heard from yourself or other people.

Your ego isn't aware of the vast world of possibilities that would enable you to attract what you want faster and easier. This is the thing that most people get caught up on—they think they know *how*. Now I don't want to dismiss a *how* if a woman here knows how to do it and has a method that's worked for her before. Then, by God, go do it. Godspeed to you.

If you have a method, a *how* that has worked for you in the past, and it's going to work this time too, then go do it, but I would remind you to be open to other ways of achieving your goal because your mind only sees this little hole of perception. The universe, your unconscious mind, Divinity sees the whole spectrum of possibilities. So if you release your little hole here and expand it a little bit and expand it a little bit more and let it get wider, you might see some other ways to accomplish and attract what you want that you never even thought of before.

So I'm not dismissing that you already have a *how*. If that's working for you and it will work for you now, do it. I say to be open to other ideas. Allow your mind to welcome different ways for things to come to you because you could be very surprised by a new *how* that is simpler than what you're already doing.

What if it doesn't work?

Someone once told me that they have tried to manifest things many times but it hasn't worked for them yet. She said, "I try to manifest a new car like you suggest, but I know that it is impossible for me to get a loan for a car because of my credit. I have tried to get loans, but they don't get through."

I've been there. When I was first learning these principles and I wanted to attract a new car, it was back when I was broke, I was unknown, and I was only learning about the law of attraction. I was driving a clunker of a car that you had to push to go anywhere, and if it broke down, it devastated me because I didn't have any money to fix it.

It was a real struggle. I was working on manifesting a new car, and every time I visualized the car that I wanted, my brain or mind would tell me, "You can't do it because your credit is bad. You don't even have a reliable job. You don't have enough money to make payments. You don't

> *"Ignore the present state and assume the wish fulfilled."*
> —Neville Goddard

even have enough money to make a down payment." My mind gave me all of the evidence why it wouldn't work.

That's what the mind does, and that's part of what this lesson is all about: learning how the brain works. Our mind is focused on the negative and I'll tell you why as we get through this lesson, but right now, it's focused on the negative.

Why is it focused on the negative? It's protecting you. It's also telling you it hasn't worked in the past, and because it didn't work in the past, it says it's not going to work in the present.

It took me a long time to get around the idea that maybe it could work for me if I can just drop all that negative thinking. You've got it made because you're reading this book and we have several more lessons. We're going to go really in deep here and we're going to clean up any negativity. We're going to erase any negative or limiting beliefs and we're going to open your mind so you have a different consciousness about what's possible.

I didn't have that. I was by myself reading books, so it took me longer. It doesn't have to take you a long time. You will attract the new car. What you have to focus on is what you really want and do your best to let the thoughts just fly by. Let them bubble up and let them disappear when they come up and say, "Hey, you can't get a loan."

That was one of the things that stopped me. I wouldn't even go to the car dealership to test-drive the car because I was convinced that I couldn't get a loan, or that I couldn't get a car; how dumb is that? I couldn't even test-drive the car because of my limiting belief. So I had to get past that and realize, wait a minute, if I want to make this car real in my life, I have to *at least* test-drive it to find out if it's what I *really* want.

So I went and test-drove the car, and I told the salesman, "I'm just looking," you know, "I'm just trying to gather everything." I also reminded myself that I don't necessarily have to buy a car. It might be given to me. I might win it. I might inherit it. There are all kinds of ways that a car can show up in your life. In fact, I've had a lot of cars over my lifetime, in the last couple decades, and I've given them away. I've had contests and somebody in my Miracle's Coaching® Program won one of my cars. They came down here and drove off with it.

A couple of my friends wanted cars, and I gave them the keys. I gave them the car. Anything can happen to bring the car to you. So you want to remain open to the idea that what was in the past doesn't equal the future.

One more thing, when I finally went to test-drive a car and I test-drove what I really liked (they had the right color and everything), they asked me to fill out the paperwork. I said, "Well it's not going to go anywhere, but I'll reluctantly do it."

I had cleared up my mind enough that when I filled out the paperwork and they took it, five hours later when I'm at home having a drink with friends, I got a call from the car dealership and they said, "You got the loan."

I said, "No, you must have the wrong person. This is Joe Vitale. I don't have credit." I barely had a job at the time and it was probably a job I didn't like.

They laughed and they said, "No, you got it and you can come pick it up."

And I did. That was my first big, big moment of attracting a new car, and I attracted it with bad credit, and no availability to get a loan. No permanent job, no reliable job, and almost no belief in myself. I must have had enough belief, because I was working on myself. I had enough belief in myself and I had *enough* belief in the possibility of the car that I manifested the car.

That, of course, opened up a whole lot of cars that have come down the road to me. So your car is coming to you. Hold the faith and focus on what you want. Don't worry about the *how*. Focus on what you want. I'll do a little meditation later about how to take inspired action that'll take you closer to bringing the car to you or you to the car.

I managed to uncover a limiting belief around money because I have been working for ten years and I haven't managed to save any money. I know that when I was growing up, money was a source of stress. How do I remove it?

This is a great question from someone we'll call Betty.

In the first lesson of this book, I touched on this. I gave two or three processes and one of them was about questioning your beliefs.

I can walk you through this right now, so it's not just Betty who has asked the question, but anybody who is trying to attract something right now and feels like there's a snag. What I want you to do is think about what you want and the frustration around not getting it. Like Betty said, she's had stress about bringing in money and she's had it ever since she was young. So whatever it is for you, stress about money, relationship help, it doesn't matter, whatever it is, see if you can think back to the very first time you had a similar thought.

In other words, right now you might be feeling the pinch when it comes to money, or you're feeling alone because you haven't attracted the relationship, but that's now. When was the first time you remember having this experience? Now, you might say it was when you were in college, which is great, or you might say when you were in high school, which is fine, but I want you to go back in your mind, go back in your memories to as early as possible.

When I was young and I was growing up, I remember my parents fighting about money. Some of the most enraged fights ever were always over a shortage of money. So as a little kid, around the age of five, I concluded there wasn't enough money and that there was a lot of stress around money.

So you want to go back to the earliest memory you can come up with and then be in that memory, be in that body of the five-year old or ten-year old, much like I was, and realize that you're making a conclusion about how the world works, based on a five-year-old person's mentality, experience, and education. So you came to a conclusion that money was stressful, or that money was scarce, or that money causes arguments, or perhaps it was that relationships were always a problem or health was always a problem.

What we're looking for is *the first cause*. So we go all the way back in our mind to the first cause, and when we find it (you can take a guess at it if you don't know for sure—I'm walking you through this process fairly quickly), when you get to that moment, realize that you're now looking at it from an adult's perspective. As an adult, what could that experience have meant?

When I saw my parents fighting when I was five years old, what else could I have concluded besides money is a problem or money causes fights? As an adult, I can make new conclusions about that experience and I can say, "Well, they had problems with money. It doesn't mean I have problems with money or anybody else has problems with money. It meant that my parents found something to fight over and if it wasn't money, it might have been something else."

It didn't necessarily have anything to do with money. So what you're doing when you go back and you reframe or retell the story of the original cause is you're freeing yourself from it.

This is a process you can do for anything, but it's certainly a process Betty can do for this particular experience. So think about that and do it on anything that's coming up.

Can changing your beliefs about a physical health problem improve health?

Absolutely yes—no hesitation. There are already books, research, scholarship, doctors, and movements proving this. I think it's Dr. Joe Dispenza who talks about this. There are a few other scientists and authors out there who talk about the power of the mind influencing your body.

One of the things to get from this book—and I'm going to be giving you a lot of advanced insights into how the world works, some of which you may never have considered before—is your mind is your body.

Author Candace Bure has written that your body is your biology. Your mind, your emotional body is your physical makeup, so you can easily change your body by changing your mind. What we're going to be talking about in this lesson is a way to do that because I'm going to walk you through the single most powerful way you can program your mind for something new for you. Whether it's a new body, relationship, health, job, money, or whatever. So the short answer is yes, you can change your health.

How do I get rid of the fear of not being good enough? I have tried many things with no success.

This is a great question because in my book, *Attract Money Now*, I say that's one of the primary fears.

People have fears about not being good enough, not being likeable, and not being approved of. You will want to take care of those.

In the last chapter, I talked about looking in the mirror. Physically go in the bathroom, look in the mirror, and start to love yourself; start to approve of yourself. Look at yourself, look at your eyes, look at your face, and find things you like. Find things you approve of and build from there.

That's a process you can do at anytime. Whenever you look in the mirror, instead of looking for some sort of disapproval or disgust or shame or embarrassment, turn it around. You are a beautiful person. You are a being of light. You are a child of the universe. Look in the mirror and feel that and say that and look at things around yourself, your body, and mind that you truly love and keep on going. Build that up. In other words, what you want to do is start loving yourself and start approving of yourself.

The Tapping Technique

While I'm on the subject, let me give you another process. I wasn't planning on talking about this one because so many people out there do it, but I love the tapping technique. The tapping technique is EFT: the *Emotional Freedom Technique.*

I learned it when it was called TFT, which was *Thought Field Therapy.* I learned TFT from the founder of Thought Field Therapy, decades ago, because he helped me get over the fear of public speaking. Of course, now I speak on *Larry King Live.* I speak in movies. I was on stage in Peru and there were 17,000 people there, live, like it was a rock concert—but in the beginning, I was terrified of speaking. I almost fainted when I spoke in front of six people one time, decades ago.

Roger Callahan created Thought Field Therapy and I learned it from him. (I also interviewed Roger Callahan once, but he's since passed away.) TFT is like psychological acupuncture. I'll share with you a quick version of it. This is the way I do it. There are a lot of books on this. There's a movie called *The Tapping Solution* that's worth seeing. I'm in it, but watch it anyway.

With tapping, you take whatever negative belief you have and tap it out. You tap on different areas of your body. You're changing your energy. You're tapping that belief out of you.

For example, someone says, "I'm not good enough." You can say anything that's bothering you. You're not smart enough. You don't feel lovable. "I'm not wealthy enough. I'm not good enough to have money," whatever it happens to be that's coming up for you.

You take that phrase and you tap on it. The way I tap is I take my left hand and I start tapping the karate chop part of my hand—the bottom part. I'm tapping it right there, I'm tapping it with a couple fingers, and I'm tapping loud enough that you should be able to hear it if I was knocking on a door. So I'm tapping fairly hard and here's what I'm saying.

"Even though I feel like I'm not good enough, I deeply love, accept, and forgive myself." So you say the phrase and add, "Even though I feel like I'm not good enough, I deeply love, accept, and forgive myself." I say it three times. "Even though I feel like I'm not good enough, (insert whatever the phrase is there), I deeply love, accept, and forgive myself."

Then I take the key words out of that phrase, and I'll say, "Not good enough" as I'm tapping the crown of my head with two fingers. I tap on the crown of my head several times.

Then I tap above my eyebrows, inside, right above my nose and eyebrows, and say, "Not good enough," while tapping pretty hard.

Next to the sides of the eyes, saying, "Not good enough." Then under the eyes, "Not good enough." Under the nose, the little cleft under the nose above the lip, "Not good enough."

Then, under the lip, right above the chin, "Not good enough," tapping it again. Then on your chest, a little soft spot about an inch under your collar bone and an inch to the left or right, "Not good enough," tapping again. Then I come back to my hand and I'm tapping between the thumb and the first finger in the little fleshy area, and I'm saying "Not good enough."

The way Roger Callahan taught it (which is different than *The Tapping Solution*) would be to close your eyes as you're still saying, "Not good enough," then open your eyes, still tapping and do a clockwise circle with your eyes, "Still not good enough." Then do a counterclockwise circle with your eyes, saying, "Not good enough," the open your eyes, close your eyes, count one, two, three, four, five, and hum "Happy Birthday." Finally, what I do is, I come down to the bottom of my hand, behind the pinky, and I tap. This is a way of closure.

So you could do the tapping sequence with anything. It could be "I don't love myself." So I'd go, "Even though I don't love myself, I deeply love, accept, and forgive myself. Even though I don't love myself, I deeply love, accept, and forgive myself." I do that three times, and then tap "don't love myself" through all of the points.

That's the tapping technique and it's one process that you can use. Again, I encourage you to read the books on it.

I have a program called *Money Beyond Belief* with Brad Yates where we do nothing but talk about tapping in regards to money. Watch the movie, *The Tapping Solution*, by Nick Ortner. He has a great book by the same name, *The Tapping Solution*.

What is a good technique to send negative thoughts away as soon as they pop up?"

I love that question. We all need to look at that. First, when we talked about this in the very first session, I said you want to start learning to watch your thoughts. You really want to get the idea that you are not your thoughts. This'll give you a sense of detachment so that when a thought comes by, you just watch it. You notice, "Oh, there's a thought, that was interesting," and just let it go, because you're not the thought. You want to be separate from the thought.

That's a process I taught in the last section, and I'm going to give you a deeper version of it about three or four lessons down the road because that's going to lead to an awakening for you. In the chapters ahead, I have some leading edge, breakthrough stuff in store for you that you're going to absolutely love.

There's another process that's worth talking about. This one is called the *What If Up* process. My friend, Mindy Audlin, talks about this and she wrote a book called *What if It All Goes Right?* It's worth reading.

Mindy says most of us have "what if down" thoughts, and this is important to realize. I said earlier that you have 60,000 to 80,000 thoughts a day. That's staggering, 60,000 to 80,000 thoughts a day. Most of them are the same thoughts and most of them are negative. So we want to detach from them. Well, what else can we do? You can *What if Up*.

So, if thoughts are "what if down," for example, you say something to the effect of, "Oh, I've heard about the tapping technique, but I don't think it's going to work for me." Well, first of all, I urge you to tap on that. "Even though I don't think the tapping technique will work on me, I deeply love, accept, and forgive myself. Even though I don't think the tapping technique would work on me..." That's the first thing I would do.

The second thing I would do is notice it's just a thought. You don't have to buy into it. It's a belief if you grab it and hold it, but it's only a thought if you let it slide by.

The third thing you can do is the *What if Up* process. If you think the tapping solution or anything isn't going to work for you, how do you feel? You feel blah, your energy drops, and you feel down. It's a downer thought. That's what's meant by "what if down."

Your thoughts are being brought down. You want to do *What if Up*. That means you change the thought into something more encouraging, more positive, more affirmative, more optimistic, more exciting, and more enthusiastic. So when a thought comes like, "Oh, that tapping technique might not work for me," turn it around. What if the tapping technique is the greatest technique of all time?

What if I'm about to teach you with *The RAS Intention Method*, here, in this particular lesson? What if this is the technique that transforms your life and you start attracting the money you want, the relationship you want, the health you want, the car you want, the job you want, the business you want, the unexpected income you want, or the joy, love, and enlightenment you want?

Notice how your energy explodes because you *What if Upped* the thought. So when thoughts come by, you don't have to buy into them. Watch them like they were just a ticker tape, or like they were graphics on a computer screen, and there they go, they're just walking on by. You don't have to buy into them at all.

You can tap the thoughts away. You can also *What if Up* thoughts. I love *What if Up* thoughts. *What if Up* is a process and a game. It is a wonderful thing to do with other people because it raises the energy of everybody in the room.

Those are some of the questions that come from working with this material and they are great questions. I love receiving your questions. I love you for sending them in to me.

Now that we have addressed questions from what we have covered thus far, let's talk about *The RAS Intention*. Do you know what RAS stands for?

It stands for your *Reticular Activating System* (RAS). Now, this is a scientific term. Maybe you've heard of it before. Some people have written about it. Maxwell Maltz wrote a book called *Psycho-Cybernetics* back in the 1960s and he called it your servomechanism. What he's referring to is the part of your brain that is operating to bring you your intentions.

Starting to get a whiff of how powerful this can be? We're talking about how the mind works. The way your mind is set up right now is in survival mode. It's set up to keep you alive. It's set up to protect you. There is nothing wrong with that and you want that. You got that from the prehistoric times so that the dinosaurs or the elephants or the wild boar or other cavemen or cavewomen or whatever was out there to get you wouldn't attack you simply because you were not aware.

Your *Reticular Activating System* has been programmed. It's hardwired in your brain to protect you. Your *Reticular Activating System* is located in the base of your brain. It's like a little knob whose job it is to keep you alive. It's based on survival.

So your brain—your mind—is operating from a survival mechanism, which also explains why anything that's worry-oriented, doubt-oriented, stress-oriented, fear-oriented is going to get your attention because it activates that part of your brain.

Your brain wants to keep you alive, which is a good thing. But your brain only focuses on survival unless you program it for something else. Now, you already know it's doing a great job at keeping you alive because you're here with me and mine is doing a great job at keeping me alive because I'm here with you. So the way it is working right now is perfect. What we want to do is get our brains to do something in addition to what it's already doing and this is where it gets exciting.

We want to program the *Reticular Activating System* (RAS) for something more. We don't want to dismiss survival, and we don't want it to short circuit that, but there is a whole lot of hard drive and software space with excess memory available, so it can have a lot more goals.

In the beginning, I asked you to choose something that you wanted to attract. I said in order for these six lessons to be of the most benefit to you, I wanted you to begin by focusing on what you want to have, do, or be. So hopefully you did that. You're allowed to change your mind as you go through the six steps because as you get more information, you'll fine-tune your goal a little bit. You'll spin it a little bit. You'll become more precise with what you want to have, do, or be and you'll also start to think bigger because you'll start to realize that you can have, do, or be anything. The only limits are the ones you believe in right now, and as you go through this, you'll start removing some of the beliefs, loosening some of the beliefs, deleting some of the beliefs, and exchanging some of the beliefs for better serving beliefs.

You may change your goal, but I need you to pick something. Now, you might have picked something and you've already changed your mind or maybe you've already attracted the thing that you wanted. Either way, I want to make sure you have something you want to have, do, or be as you continue to move forward.

Whatever your desire, big or small, it should be something that's a stretch for you, and something that will convince you that all of this is working. It should not be something that feels impossible because if it feels impossible to you, you're not going to try that hard because you'll bump into the ceiling of what you think is possible (a belief). Until you get all this information in you, we have to slowly dissect the beliefs, and then remove them. Then you can start entertaining the idea of having more of the things you really, authentically, honestly want for yourself.

For now, start with something you want. I'll give you a second to think about that.

Setting an RAS Intention

All right, I hope you've got something written down because what we're going to do is set an intention using your *Reticular Activating System*.

This is fantastic. I can't tell you how excited I am about this because I have achieved a heck of a lot. I told you earlier about some of the stuff in my life, but I know tens of thousands of people, people who read my books, people who watch my movies, people who listen to my self-help music, people who in one shape or another practice this material. Whether they're winning a lottery for $40 million dollars or finding the love of their lives or getting their dream job or opening up their business or becoming a bestselling author, they're achieving their dreams. I want you to achieve your dreams next.

We want to set and achieve a goal using the *Reticular Activating System*. How do you do this? Three ways. This is the three-step formula and I feel compelled to read one line from a book called *The Great Within*, published in 1907 by Christian D. Larson.

He said, "the proper conditions for recording an impression upon the subconscious are deep feeling, strong desire, conscious interest, and a living faith." When he said, "you're implanting it in your subconscious mind," he's referring to where the *Reticular Activating System* is actually operating.

You may not be consciously aware of it, or you may not have consciously even heard of it, but that RAS is in the base of your brain and it's attached to and working with your subconscious mind. Christian Larson and all the new thought and law of attraction authors, all the way up to and including me, have been talking about how to influence the *Reticular Activating System* without knowing that it was called the *Reticular Activating System*.

Butterfly Example

The three things that you have to have with your goal are: to be emotional; to be vivid, graphic, and add imagery; and to repeat it. Let me explain.

I'm a lifetime member of The Society of American Magicians and I gave a presentation to The Society of American Magicians Conference this past year (2015) in Austin, Texas (USA). I began by asking, "How many butterflies do you see in the room?"

Well, they were in a giant conference room. There were no butterflies. Then I went on to say:

Well, if you started to get emotionally involved with butterflies, like they were the love of your life; you were passionate about butterflies and you collected books and photos and websites and all kinds of information about butterflies, and you really had a driving passion for butterflies, you'd be sending that message to your RAS, to your subconscious mind, and it would take note.

Then if you added imagery: If you started looking at butterflies or you went walking through the woods or through the forest or you went to parks or you went to environments where there were a lot of butterflies and you just looked at the images of them and you loved butterflies—you have the emotion, love is there, and now you have the image, the graphics, and the visuals are there. You are double whamming the brain, the Reticular Activating System.

Then if you repeat this, if you do this every day, if you thought about butterflies, loved butterflies, looked at photos of butterflies and you did that every day, you would program a new command in your Reticular Activating System. *You will have implanted a new goal, desire, or job, etc. with your subconscious mind.*

When I was at that magician's convention I told them about butterflies.

I said, "Right now you're on alert for butterflies because I mentioned butterflies, but unless you repeat this later today or tomorrow or the next day, you're going to forget all about butterflies and you'll forget that I brought it up and this is the key to making this process work."

Your Goal and the RAS

What I need you to do in order to activate the *Reticular Activating System* for a new goal for you is to choose that goal. Remember, I said pick one thing that you want to have, do, or be.

1. Feel the Love

Then find the passion for it, find the joy in it, and find the love for it. You see, we tend to manifest things we love, fear, or hate because they're strong emotions and the emotions go into our mind. We don't want to attract things that we fear or we hate, so we want to focus on love. Find what you love, what you feel good about, what you're joyful about for the thing you want to have, do, or be. That's the first step.

In fact, I'm going to pause for a second for you to imagine what would it feel like to have what you want. Feel that joyful feeling. If it is a car, what would it feel like? Feel the joy of owning that car or having that relationship; how would that feel? Pick something that you feel fantastic in imagining.

2. Picture It

Then what we want to do is add some imagery around it. In your mind's eye, to the best of your ability, can you see it? We want a graphic representation of your desire.

You might find magazine articles and clip out some photos. People do that when they want to change their bodies, for example. They will go and find a younger, slimmer, healthier, stronger version of themselves or they'll go find an actor or actresses' photo that they want to look like or they want to resemble. What they're doing is finding the image to go with the emotion that activates the *Reticular Activating System*. Are you with me here?

In your mind, conjure up an image—and I know some people say they can't see things in their mind. For now, just feel it. Later go and find a graphic or a photo or something that has an image you can look at. For example, if you were in love with butterflies, you'd be feeling how much you love butterflies, but you'd also be finding images of butterflies online or in photo books or something. So do that now.

3. Repeat

Now, you have something you love—you passionately want this and you can feel it. You feel how great it would be to have it. Then you see it. See yourself having it or see the product or see the service or see some aspect that represents what you want. Excellent. Then the third thing is repeating it. In other words, you would do this process every day.

You can do it as many times a day as you like, but the prime times that everybody agrees on over the last century is right when you're going to sleep and right when you're waking up in the morning. So, as you're going to sleep at night, you're lying in bed and you're getting comfortable and you're sighing because the day is done. That's when you want to conjure up the feeling.

"Oh, I really want the Mercedes Gullwing 300SL" or "I really want the job."

But don't focus on want because that's kind of hinting at a lack. You focus on the feeling of having it. It's almost like Nevillizing your goal, which I will discuss later and we'll be talking about more as we go through these lessons. What you want to do is feel as if you've already achieved it. What's the joy in driving the car? What's the joy in having the romance? What's the joy in having the business?

Whatever it is, feel the joy, feel the love as you're going to sleep. Then in your mind, see the image. You see the butterflies or the car or the money or the beaches in Maui, or whatever it is that you want. See it in your mind's eye and feel it in your body. Repeat it as you go to sleep. When you wake up in the morning, repeat it then.

Those are the three ways to activate the system.

Doing this, your brain isn't only working on survival. It still has to keep you alert; it still has to protect you, but now it's focused on helping you attract something you want to experience in your life. Pretty cool, huh?

Segment Intending

Segment Intending is another process that I want to quickly share with you because this is a way of getting through your day with a whole lot more power.

What most of us do is set a goal for a week or a month or a year (if we set goals at all). I do believe in the power of intention. I also think there's something more powerful than intention and in the later lessons we'll get to that because it's breakthrough material. It'll make intentions seems wimpy compared to what we're going to be talking about later in this book, but intentions are better than being a victim.

Most people walk through lives just bouncing off circumstances, and reacting unconsciously. They're not awake or alive or aware at all. They're not expecting miracles, they're expecting the worst and they generally get it. So you want to have intentions to carry you through and move you in the right direction. Segment

Intending means you divide up your day into many intentions.

For example, when I wake up in the morning, before I get out of bed or as I'm getting out of bed, I swing my legs over and sit on the side of the bed and I state my first intention. I intend to wake up clear-headed, stretch, feeling fantastic, and go have my coffee. Then I intend to go have a fantastic workout where I feel stronger than ever before and I lift more and I bend more and I do more than ever. What I'm doing is breaking down the moments almost hour by hour.

With Segment Intending, you can break it down into minutes. For example, before I prepared this chapter, there were a bunch of things I had to do. I had to set up a computer. I had to make sure I had my water. I had to make sure the phone was turned off and other things were turned off that won't distract me, but I also realized that as I write to you, I don't have a script.

I am writing completely from inspiration. There isn't anybody queuing me about what to put on the page. All I have is what you're looking at on the screen or in your hands. Segment Intending is an excellent system to break down the mind's resistance. The rest of this is coming from inspiration through me to you. So before I began this section, I stated my segment intended. I said that I want to be clear and present and be of the most help, the most inspiration, and the most information to you.

I stated an intention for this time. That's how Segment Intending works. For example, let's say you go on a job interview tomorrow morning and you pull into the office building and you're in the car. Before you get out of the car, you say to yourself, "I intend to go in there and be my best, show my best, and get this job or something better." I always add the phrase "or something better" to my intentions because, again, my ego doesn't see the world of possibilities and the universe does. So I don't want to block the universe from greater good coming to me because of an intention that's a limitation.

So Segment Intending is an excellent system to break down the mind's resistance—the mind is still going to be coming from fear because it's programmed to look for things to be afraid of. It's your Reticular Activating System doing its job. But now you've asked the Reticular Activating System (RAS) to do something else—to help you to have, do, or be whatever it is that you're looking for next.

One way to help your RAS along is to break down your moments into intentions. So when you're about to go on a blind date or you're about to meet somebody new, before you get out of the car, before you go into the restaurant, before you have the drink, state your intention. What do you want to have happen? What do you want to experience? You intend something for that segment of the day.

You can do this all day long and it's a fun process. Do it with a spirit of letting go. You're about to go home. You're about to get in traffic. You intend for the traffic to be light, and for you to get home faster and safer than ever. That would be intending something for that segment (the drive home from work). That's how you use Segment Intending.

The Five-Step System

This is the Five-Step System for manifesting virtually anything. This system is so powerful and so exciting to me; it is also very close to my heart. This is the system I've been using for a couple decades or more. I wrote about it in my book, *The Attractor Factor*. So if you already read *The Attractor Factor*, you're probably somewhat familiar with it, but I want to go through the five-step system here, because it really can help us to manifest miracles.

Now, in a way, we've been doing it over these first couple lessons, but I want to make sure that you really hone in on this particular process because this is powerful.

The first step in the five-step system is to *know what you don't want*. Most people start there and stop there because all they do is complain. They say "I don't want taxes, I don't want to be broke, I don't want to be alone, I don't want to have hangovers, I don't want to have insomnia, I don't want to..." just fill in the blank.

They're just complaining; but I use that first step, know what you don't want, to get to **the second step**, *know what you **do** want*. In other words, you use your complaint and turn it into your intention. So if you said, "I'm tired of driving my clunker car; I don't want to drive a beat-up car anymore." Your intention would be: "I intend to attract, own, and drive a car I absolutely love that works fantastic, looks fantastic, and that's paid for in full."

Or if you say in the first step, "I don't want to be alone anymore." Then the second step would be turning that into what you do want. "I want to find the love of my life. I want to find my soul mate or I want to find somebody to date that I love and have so much in common with that it's a hoot to get together every time." Do you see what I'm doing? The first step is to *know what don't you want*. You use that to declare *what you DO want*.

You can pick something right now. Find whatever it is you've been complaining about, that's the first step, that's what you don't want. Turn it into your intention. "I don't want to be unhappy. I intend to be happy." Those are the first two steps.

The third step is huge. We're not going to go through it in detail right now, but the good news is I'm going to spend the entire next lesson on it. The next lesson is called clearing. *Clearing* is the most important thing. As I told you in the last chapter, clearing is the missing secret to having what you want.

Clearing is the missing secret to virtually all the self-help programs, and self-improvement books and courses that are out there. There may be some exceptions, but in my experience, they don't talk about clearing. Clearing is getting rid of the counterintentions, the negative beliefs, the limiting beliefs, the negativity, the data, the memories, the programs, the mind shift, all of the stuff that is negative that is bringing you down and blocking your good from you. You have to be clear of that.

For the longest time I was doing all the right things. I thought I was setting my intentions and visualizing and scripting and doing all this stuff, but I wasn't getting what I wanted and it's because that third step wasn't there. The getting clear step. You must get clear to have, do, or be what you want.

Now, again, the third lesson is all about getting clear and I'm going to give you processes to get clear and you're going to love it. What I tell everybody is when you get clear you will have what you want because there won't be anything blocking it. The only things blocking what you want right now are your hidden beliefs. I know you don't know that or feel that or even believe that, but you have hidden beliefs in your unconscious mind.

In that subconscious mind, the hidden database of beliefs, you have a warehouse of beliefs and limitations that are preventing you from having what you want. So, **the third step** in the five-step system *is to get clear*. We're going to do nothing but clearing in the next lesson.

The fourth step is to *Nevillize your goal*. Neville Goddard is one of my favorite authors, and he has written a lot of books including *Feeling is the Secret*. Most people refer to him as just Neville. I coined the word "Nevillize" and that's where you take what it is that you want to have, do, or be, and pretend that you've already attracted it, that it's already over, and you feel what it's like to actually experience the completion of the idea.

That's Nevillizing your goal. I have provided an experiential exercise on *Nevillizing Your Goal* at the end of this chapter that you can use for all of your intentions. But to give you a taste of what to expect, pick something that you want to have, do, or be. Instead of pushing it off in the distance where you're going to have it sometime down the road, imagine that it happened today.

You got the car this morning. You drove it this afternoon. You went out on your date this afternoon and you had a great time. You got the new job and you got the raise today. Feel that as if it actually happened today. Feel it in your body and mind.

When you truly get to that point where you believe it, you've Nevillized your goal. That means, first of all, you sent it into your Reticular Activating System. Your brain just went online and said, "Oh, we need to manifest that because she's already saying she's got it."

So Nevillizing activates the Reticular Activating System. It also sends out an order to the universe, to the field of all possibilities, to the Divine, or to whatever you want to call the great something that we're all a part of. Because you Nevillized it, it's a thought form that now goes out from your body into the world. This is powerful.

You can do that process any time. Just take a few seconds and imagine you achieved the very thing you wanted to achieve. It happened. What does it feel like? Excellent. Just experience what it feels like to already have it instead of thinking, "Oh, I want it." What would it be like if you said, "Oh, I already have it"?

The fifth step of the five-step system for manifesting virtually anything is to *let go while taking inspired action*.

Letting go while taking inspired action means that you let go of your addiction or your attachment or your need for it to happen in a particular way. This is where you add the phrase "…this or something better."

So if you said, "I really want to have a BMW car" and you have the model and color, you would end it by saying "...this or something better." You'll leave that little loophole for the universe to present some better good to you.

The fifth step is all about not needing things to work out in a particular way. When you need something to work out a particular way, there's a sense of desperation behind you, which is tipping a belief that you really don't believe it's going to happen, else why would you be so desperate about it? You want to come more from faith and you're taking inspired action in this same sense.

The fifth step has two parts to it. You're letting go, letting go of any need, and you take inspired action. That means when you have a feeling to do something, inspiration comes to you, intuition comes to you, or you're presented with an opportunity that feels in your gut that it's relevant, you must act on it. That's the fifth step and it's very important because the number one thing that people overlook is taking inspired action.

They want to sit, they want to visualize, they want to fantasize, but they don't want to get up and do anything. What I have found out is that life is a co-creation. You have to do your part. You're an energy-being in a dance with other energy-beings. We're dancing right now together. Our energies are dancing and we're creating something together because our energies are dancing.

So you want to let go of any need or addiction for things to work out and you want to take inspired action. Act on whatever might be leading you to the very thing you said you wanted. Those are the five steps.

Guided Meditation

Now, I have a treat for you. It is an *inspired action meditation*. In audio format, it's ten minutes long. Reading the written version may be different. You can read it aloud to yourself (and even record it) and it will help you take inspired action. This is important and relevant because a lot of people don't take inspired action. A lot of people just sit around and wait for everything to happen—the phone to ring, the doorbell to ring—and those do happen. Miracles do happen all the time and we want to expect miracles, but we also want to co-create miracles. We do that by taking inspired action.

This short meditation is from a longer series called *Attract Money Now Meditations*. I made the audio CD with Mathew Dixon (see http://guitarmonks.com/amnm/) who made the music, while I provided the audio narration meditation. All you have to do is relax and listen to it. If you do not have the audio, simply relax and read this meditation to yourself.

Request from the Universe an Inspired Action

This is a short meditation on requesting from the universe an inspired action.

Now just relax. Be sure you're in a place where you will not be disturbed. You should not be driving. Your phone should be off. You should be sure that you're going to be uninterrupted. You can sit. You can lie down. You can close your eyes or you can leave them open. It's entirely up to you how quickly you relax. Now breathe deeply and let it go slowly. You feel yourself relax. As I count from ten to one, you'll feel your body relax even more.

Your mind will relax even more and you can focus on my voice as you ease into this state of tranquility… of tranquility.

Ten, please forgive me… please forgive me.

Nine, I'm sorry…I'm sorry.

Eight, thank you…thank you.

Seven, I love you…I love you.

Six, relaxing more and more…relaxing more and more.

Five, letting go of all stress…letting go of all stress.

Four, focused on my voice…focused on my voice.

Three, relaxing even more…relaxing even more.

Two, letting go…letting go.

One, totally relaxed…totally relaxed.

However you feel, whatever is going on in your body or your mind, is totally fine. As you continue to relax, you know that you can talk to the universe. You can make a request. You have goals. You have desires. You have things you want. Things you have to have, do, or be. Things you want to experience. Take note of your goals in your own mind. Just be playful and be relaxed.

And now, either out loud or in your mind, make a request. Say "universe, please show me what to do next."

Universe, please give me a sign.

Universe, please show me the way.

You can make this request of your unconscious mind of the Divine, of nature. You are free to use whatever words feel right to you. You know you are co-creating your reality. You are asking for assistance. So ask of the world, please show me the next steps.

Please give me an indication of what to do.

Please help me see the action I'm inspired to take next.

You may get an answer in the next moment or you may get an answer later today or tonight or tomorrow. Allow the answer to come at its own pace. But be expectant. You know you will receive an inspiration. You know that even if you don't know where that inspiration will take you, it's the right thing to do next.

You know to trust inspiration. You know to take action. You know following your guidance is the wise thing to do to attract more money now. You trust yourself. You trust your guidance. You trust the universe and you take action on inspired ideas even when you don't know how they will work out.

You trust the process. You trust yourself. You trust the universe. Inspiration is a gift from the Divine.

And now let's come back to your normal waking consciousness. Easily and smoothly. Take in a deep breath and let it out. And as I count from one to ten, you will become more and more awake, and more and more alert.

One, I love you…I love you.

Two, I'm sorry…I'm sorry.

Three, please forgive me…please forgive me.

Four, thank you…thank you.

Five, you can stretch a little if you'd like…if you'd like.

Six, then open your eyes if they're not opened yet…not opened yet.

Seven, get another deep breath and let it go…and let it go.

Eight, aware of where you are, aware of my voice, aware of the room you're in.

Nine, becoming fully awake and fully awake.

Ten, you are now wide-awake; feeling great. Looking forward to your day with expectation and knowing you are now attracting more money.

Now we have covered the five-step process. The last step being let go and take inspired action.

―――

The Three-Day Rule

I mentioned the *Three-Day Rule* in the first lesson. The Three-Day Rule is dealing with the reality that, generally speaking, you're going to manifest whatever you're thinking and feeling right now in about three days. It's a general rule of thumb.

Now, why doesn't that happen all the time? If you think and feel something right now, why doesn't it always show up in three days? It is because you're having 80,000 thoughts a day. Most of them negative, most of them limiting, and most of them the same thoughts. Obviously you're not maintaining the thinking and feeling intention for it to hatch in three days. I want you to be aware of the Three-Day Rule because this is an insight.

When you state an intention, which you've done today and in the first lesson, a lot of the counter beliefs start showing up. Unless you take care of those, you'll slow down the process of manifesting what you want. You now have a lot more tools and a lot more processes to help you so that you can manifest what you want within three days.

The next chapter is going to be extremely important, extremely powerful, and empowering to help you to be able to manifest faster because it's the lesson on getting clear. It's the one on erasing counterintentions. But first, a few more techniques to learn.

Scripting

I want to make sure I serve you the best I can, so I want to mention the scripting process. *Scripting* is a process where you sit down and you write out your script, your intention, as if it's already happened. So it's a little bit like Nevillizing in writing. What you're doing is being a playwright for your life.

Instead of writing, "I want more income by next week," and putting it out there in the universe as a distant reality, you pretend you already have it. "Today, I attracted $5,000 in unexpected income! It was an amazing surprise to me! I couldn't stop smiling! I felt like my heart was going to explode through my chest! I have Christmas lights going on in my brain!" Whatever it is.

What you're doing is scripting the excitement of achieving and attracting your goal. This is another way to activate the Reticular Activating System in your brain.

Why are you activating it this way? Mostly because of emotion. When you're writing out your scripting and Nevillizing, you're writing the very thing you want, as if you've already attracted it. You are powerfully pulling a lever in your RAS system and turning it on.

It's almost like you just flipped a switch and turned on a computer command center in your brain. It's now getting flooded with emotion from the scripting. So find time to do scripting. All you have to do is get a notebook. You can do it on the computer, but doing it in your own handwriting seems to be more powerful because it's a sensory connection to your whole body and right to your brain. Writing in longhand is the first way of communicating with our own brain.

The Remembering Process

The Remembering Process is a wonderful tool that's a fantastic process itself. Daniel Barrett, who's my music producer on my singer/songwriter albums, told me about The Remembering Process, and together we wrote a book on it that Hay House published.

The essence of it is like an advanced visualization technique. Most people, when they visualize something, they sit here and they visualize the new car, the health, or the romance off in the distance, like some day they're going to have it. With The Remembering Process, you go ahead of that visualization to the future and you remember back to the moment when you actually manifested it.

Let that can sink in because this is a very different process than what most people are used to.

When I first started going into the studio with Daniel Barrett, and I told him I was struggling with writing songs, he said, "It's easier to remember than it is to create." I thought, *What does that mean? It's easier to remember than it is to create.* It made no sense to me.

Then he said, "Instead of trying to sit here and create a song, why don't you imagine the song is already written and try to remember it?"

That really spun my head around a little bit, but I started to play with the idea. So instead of visualizing that I'm *going* to write a song, I visualized that I *already did* write a song, and it was in the past, and I imagined what the song might be like. I tried to remember it. So you could do the same thing.

You could use the process that follows.

You are trying to attract something right now or achieve something, so you're focused on it. Instead of imagining that it's not yet created, you imagine that it was already created in the future at some point. We'll say three months from now. Well, in your mind, you go five months out, and try to remember to that three-month point, and you play with the idea that you already manifested and attracted the miracle.

Then, you try to remember how you did it so that you can tell the present you in this moment some new ways to actually create it. Now again, I know this is an advanced concept, but sit with it a little bit. If you get a chance, pick up the book. I'm not necessarily telling you to buy it. Go to the library and borrow the book called *The Remembering Process* by Daniel Barrett and me.

Again, the idea is to imagine that what you want is already accomplished in the future and you go further out in the future and remember back to the moment when you created it.

Another way to look at this is to pretend there's a parallel universe. There's another earth and there's *another you*, and on that other earth, it's six months ahead of this point in time. So on the other earth six months out, the *other you* already manifested what you're trying to manifest now.

So imagine *your other you* did it and try to imagine how you did it. You're remembering what you did, because you did it in the future, as a way to help you manifest it in this present moment. That's a good one to work with.

Healing Music

I'd like to briefly share with you how to use healing music to clear your past beliefs. I'd like you to visit the site http://www.cdbaby.com/cd/onemoreday so you can sample one of my songs. It's called *Some Thoughts*.

Some Thoughts is a great reminder that some thoughts are great and some thoughts really suck. It'll help remind you that you have a juke box in your brain and if you don't like the thought, you change it like you change a song. You just ask for the next one. So it's a way of teaching you how to use your brain.

There are a lot of levels to healing music. I call myself the world's first self-help singer/songwriter because I noticed that a lot of music like the Rolling Stones' famous song from the 1960s about *You Can't Always Get What You Want* were programming us. They were programming us and you and I didn't know it.

Then we become adults and we go, "Hey, I can't always get what I want," not realizing the Rolling Stones sang it right into our heads. They sang it right into our Reticular Activating System. It was catchy, it was memorable, it had energy, it had imagery, and they repeated it. That's how it works.

So I wanted to create music that was positive and healing. Of course, there are other people creating self-help and healing music too.

I wrote a little book called Healing Music. It's free. It's at healingmusicbook.com. You can just go read it, it doesn't cost anything. I hope you will gain a sense of what singing and music can do.

This has been an amazing chapter to share with you. I am going to close this chapter with a few questions that I have received from others at this point in their six-step journey. I believe the questions and answers will be helpful to you. Enjoy.

Common Questions

If you want to work for a specific partner, do you work on any one or do you work on a specific person?

That's a great question. The number one question I get almost every day from somebody is how do I attract my next door neighbor or my boss or how do I get my lover back or how do I get my spouse back?

It's a number one question and they're all doing it wrong because it is a violation of free will to try to attract a particular person. Never focus on attracting a particular person. The wiser approach, the more loving approach, the more divine approach is to focus on attracting a person who has the qualities that you like in whoever it is you've been thinking about.

I have a friend who, years ago, was looking for her soul mate. She came into a Mastermind Group I was in and she had a long list of all the qualities she was looking for in a soul mate. There was nowhere on that list a name of a particular person, but she was looking for somebody who was kind, who was a great conversationalist, who was charming, who had great sense of humor, and so on. She had thirty or so items on the list. She focused on the qualities she wanted.

Two months later, she found the person who had twenty-five of the thirty-six or so qualities. They started dating, they got married, and they are traveling around the world as happy as can be. She found her soul mate.

Anybody can do this, but we do not want to lock in on a specific person.

You write down the qualities that you like or admire in others and identify what you want. That's what you're going to focus on and Nevillize and script and remember and activate the Reticular Activating System with. It will then go out there. Remember, there are seven billion people on the planet. Surely there's somebody out there that has all the qualities you're looking for. Leave it to the universe to help bring that person to you and you to them. Remember to take inspired action; much like that meditation guided you to do.

I have heard the term let go a lot. How does that fit into the emotions repeated over and over again?

What you're doing is you're feeling it but with a sense of play. A friend of mine says the question we should all ask is, "Wouldn't it be cool if I attracted...?" then fill in the blank.

In other words, there's no need; there's no desperation. Most of us demand it to be a certain way and we must have it, thus we don't have a spirit of letting go. We want to go through our imagery and our emotion and our repetition with a sense of play.

For example, "Wow, wouldn't it be cool if I got that new car?" or, "Wow, wouldn't it be cool if I started dating that person that the universe brings to me?" (not one who you go and find yourself).

"Wouldn't it be cool if you started to attract the money into your life?" There's a deep sense of faith that you're going to do it for the highest good of all concerned and with a true lack of desperation. You can let go easily if you're not desperate. You're letting go of a need. It's a psychological thing. You're coming from a place of faith. So I really think we have two choices. You come from fear or you come from faith. Most people come from fear—I know I have, and I'm sure you have too.

We want to come from faith. We want to come from the idea that all of this stuff works and we truly *expect miracles*. As a result of that, of course, we're going to relax because it's all going to work out and, in fact, it's already working out.

My mind has a kind of resistance to this process. I want to do it and then I don't. Why and what can I do?

That's totally fine. What you want to do is whatever process is most fun for you. I've been giving you a lot of different processes. I gave you some in the last chapter and I gave you several in this one. Pick one that feels fun for you. This doesn't need to be work and, in fact, if it feels like work, then we're doing something wrong. It should be like fun.

You should be excited to say, "Oh, for the next thirty minutes, I'm going to intend that I focus on good thoughts or over the next hour I'm going to start the *What if Up* process." Or maybe Nevillizing is what really excites you and you really just start to sit and experience what it's like to already have what you want to attract in the future. You pretend that you have it now.

Also, look at the idea that you are okay with having things be better. Are you okay having things be better? Are you okay with your good being increased, because if you aren't, it's a sign that you haven't approved of yourself yet or you don't fully love yourself yet, because you do deserve to have it better. You do deserve to have great good. You do deserve to *expect miracles*.

So, you may have to start there.

I also gave you the tapping technique. If you feel like there's a sense of lack of approval or a lack of self-love or lack of self-worth, start with "I feel like I don't truly love myself right now. So even though I don't truly love myself right now, I deeply love, accept, and forgive myself." Then go through the whole tapping process.

I assure you that in the pages ahead, we're going to be going through some processes that you're going to love because all of these are opening our minds, opening our hearts, and plugging us in, right in to the current of the universe.

Your Turn: Nevillize Your Goal Meditation

Earlier, I mentioned a process called *Nevillizing Your Goal*. Nevillizing is very powerful. I have talked about it in a lot of my books, especially *The Attractor Factor*. Neville Goddard talked about not just visualizing what you want to have happen, but to actually feel it as being complete. You embody the experience of what you desire as if it took place today. On the following pages, I'm going to walk you through a ten-minute *Nevillize Your Goal Meditation* that I would normally do live or on audio. You can read along with the meditation, or you can read it aloud and record it for yourself to listen to. (I will note where to start and stop your recording.)

Before we begin, pick a goal that you want to manifest or achieve. Choose something you would like to have, do, or be for this exercise. It could be the very intention you said you wanted earlier or in this lesson. You're going to imagine that it actually came to pass. Imagine that you actually finalized it and fulfilled it and it happened yesterday or it happened this morning and you're super excited about it.

When you Nevillize, you want to actually feel it. I wrote a song on my latest singer-songwriter album *One More Day* called "Feel it Real." That's what you're doing. You're feeling it real. This is a way to bypass beliefs and melt down counterintentions by leapfrogging past them all. You go right to the end result. You don't imagine that your goal is going to happen next week or next month, you actually feel like it happened today. How cool is that?

Now, let's begin our *Nevillize Your Goal Meditation*.

Nevillize Your Goal Meditation

(Start Your Recording Now)

Now just relax. Be sure you're in a place where you will not be disturbed. You should not be driving. Your phone should be off. You should be sure that you're going to be uninterrupted. You can sit. You can lie down. You can close your eyes or you can leave them open. It's entirely up to you how quickly you relax.

Now breathe deeply and let it go slowly. You feel yourself relax. As I count from ten to one, you'll feel your body relax even more. Your mind will relax even more and you can focus on my voice as you ease into this state of tranquility.

Ten. Please forgive me. Please forgive me. Please forgive me. Please forgive me.

Nine. I'm sorry. I'm sorry. I'm sorry. I'm sorry.

Eight. Thank you. Thank you. Thank you.

Seven. I love you. I love you. I love you.

Six. Relaxing more and more. Relaxing more and more. Relaxing more and more.

Five. Letting go of all stress. Letting go of all stress. Letting go of all stress.

Four. Focused on my voice. Focused on my voice. Focused on my voice. Focused on my voice.

Three. Relaxing even more. Relaxing even more. Relaxing even more. Relaxing even more.

Two. Letting go. Letting go. Letting go.

One. Totally relaxed. Totally relaxed. Totally relaxed.

However you feel, whatever is going on in your body or your mind is totally fine ... is totally fine ... is totally fine ... is totally fine.

And now as you relax, allow your mind to drift into the future. You go to the place where your goals have already been achieved. Maybe you wanted unexpected income, well it's already happened.

What does that feel like? What do you tell yourself? What do you tell others when you explain the wonderful way your unexpected income has come about? Or maybe you desired a better job and now you have it. It's already come to pass. You can feel it. You can see it. Perhaps you call a friend and say, "I have the job." What do you tell the friend? How does that feel? What do you tell yourself inside? Perhaps you wanted to increase sales in your business online or off. It's happened.

As you look at yourself in the future, you see these goals have already come to pass. It's amazing. It's miraculous. It's wonderful. What do you tell yourself? How do you feel? What do you tell other people about your goals coming true?

And as you look in the future, what else do you notice? What wonderful things have also happened that surprised you? Now that you have a better relationship with money, now that you truly love yourself, appreciate yourself, and know that you deserve all good things, how much more do you smile? How much happier do you feel? What else do you tell people about these miracles happening in your life?

And as you continue to relax, these future visualizations are anchoring in your unconscious mind. They're planted and they have come true. They come to you in unexpected ways. Ways that surprise you, delight you, ways that you want to celebrate. Imagine in the future the money you wanted is there. You can see it. You can feel it. You can touch it. You call a friend to share the good news about how you attracted more money now. What do you tell your friend? What do you tell yourself?

You've become so accustomed to the money appearing in your life, that this is your new way of being. This is how you think. This is how you act. You've become an inspiration to others. You are a wealthy, successful, healthy, and happy person.

And now let's come back to your normal waking consciousness. Easily and smoothly. Take in a deep breath and let it out. As I count from one to ten, you will become more and more awake and more and more alert.

One, I love you...I love you.

Two, I'm sorry... I'm sorry...I'm sorry.

Three, please forgive me... please forgive me...please forgive me.

Four, thank you... thank you...thank you.

Five, you can stretch a little if you'd like...if you'd like.

Six, then open your eyes if they're not opened yet...not opened yet.

Seven, give another deep breath and let it go...and let it go.

Eight, aware of where you are, aware of my voice, aware of the room you're in.

Nine, becoming fully awake and fully alert.

Ten, you are now wide-awake, feeling great. Looking forward to your day with expectation and knowing you are now attracting more money.

(You can stop your recording now.)

Excellent. Now just take a deep breath and relax. Let that exercise sink in. That's Nevillizing your goal; you are acting as if it has already taken place.

A Gentle Reminder

As this chapter comes to a close, I want to remind you that the way to activate the Reticular Activating System is to focus on what you want, but to focus on it with love. Find the true, positive emotion for it. Then you also want to find the image that represents it and be able to look at it. Then third, you want to repeat this. With those three steps, this one process alone will activate your subconscious mind to plan a new goal or a new activity in your brain to work on.

Then it will start sorting out the millions of bits of information in the world, selecting what's relevant to your new goal, and then it'll make you consciously aware of it. So the Reticular Activating System, that reticular activating intention, I think this is one of the most powerful things that I've talked about in a long time. The key points, of course, are focusing on emotion, focusing on imagery, and focusing on repetition.

Keep in mind that I've given you a lot of other processes from *The Five-Step Formula* for attracting whatever you want, to *Nevillizing Your Goal*, to *Scripting*, to *The Remembering Process*, to the *What if Up?* process. This is a smorgasbord; this is a buffet of different techniques, all of which work, but what's really exciting is in the next chapter we're going to do the counterintention clearing. Again, for me, this is the most important thing.

As I guide you through the clearing process, I will be sending you energy, and we will be melting resistance in real time. This is very powerful; this is very exciting, and I can't stress enough—it's the missing secret. It's the missing secret to having what you want. You want to get clear of those counterintentions. Remember intentions are what you consciously say you want. Counterintentions are what the unconscious mind and subconscious are throwing up as the objections.

In fact, one thing you can start doing is paying attention to your own objections. Yes, there are parts of you that are resisting some of this. Those are counterintentions. They are demonstrating the parts of you that need to be cleared. The next chapter, the third lesson, is Counterintention Clearing. You're going to love it.

Again, I love you. I am proud of you. I am so grateful for you. Keep doing this great work. Participate and work on all the different processes we've discussed, and remember our new mantra, *expect miracles, expect miracles*. I'll see you in the next chapter. Enjoy the words to the song *Some Thoughts* and listen to it online.

SOME THOUGHTS

Words and Music ©2015 by Joe Vitale. All rights reserved.
www.AllHealingMusic.com

some thoughts
make you happy
some thoughts
make you sad
some thoughts
make you angry
some thoughts
make you glad

some thoughts
make you crazy
some thoughts
make you mild
some thoughts
make you lazy
some thoughts
make you wild

Ohhh ohhh ohhh

> like a jukebox in your mind
> you can change the song any time
> choose the thought that makes you free
> choose the thought that makes you happy

some thoughts
are crappy
some thoughts
are wise
some thoughts
are snappy
some thoughts
are cries

some thoughts
are loving
some thoughts
are strong
some thoughts
are joyful
some thoughts
are wrong

Ohhh ohhh ohhh

> like a jukebox in your mind
> you can change the song any time
> choose the thought that makes you free
> choose the thought that makes you happy

> like a jukebox in your mind
> you can change the song any time
> choose the thought that makes you free
> choose the thought that makes you happy

like a jukebox in your mind
you can change the song any time
choose the thought that makes you free
choose the thought that makes you happy

like a jukebox in your mind
you can change the song any time
choose the thought that makes you free
choose the thought that makes you happy

whoa, what he said!

STEP THREE

Counterintention Clearing

*It is our interpretation of the past, our limiting
beliefs, and our undigested pain that stop us from
being able to move forward with clear direction.*
—Debbie Ford

Welcome to step three in our six-step process. This is midway. There's so much we've done and so much yet to do. I want to be sure we applaud and congratulate you because you're doing something fantastic for yourself. You're working on yourself, you're growing, you're learning, you're expanding, you're stretching, and your consciousness is changing as we're going through these lessons. Just imagine what's going to happen by the time we go through all six of these! It's going to be a transformation.

The whole process is called *The Miracle* and by the time we're done, you're going to be seeing miracles everywhere you turn because the reality is *miracles are here*. We typically don't see them because of the filters, or the belief systems that we have—most of which we get from well-meaning parents around us—that were downloaded and wired before we could even sing and walk and dance and talk. But we can do something about that now because we're conscious beings taking control of our lives. That's what you're doing now and that's why I want to acknowledge you.

Congratulations on Your Progress

I'm proud of you. I'm excited for you and I'm very excited about this particular lesson, because we're doing the counterintention clearing. You've heard me talk about this because I said having intentions is powerful. You want to have intentions, but what most people don't know, which I say is the missing secret, is that you must clear the counterintentions, negative beliefs, and limiting beliefs, whether you know them or not, that are in your unconscious mind. And that's what this particular session is all about.

I'm going to bring my entire arsenal here and I'm going to be sending energy to you. I'm actually going to pause at one point and I'm going to be sending energy to you because I do Reiki and Qigong energy. I am an Esoteric Energy Practitioner and I'll be sending that to you. We're also going to be doing some processes, maybe some you've never heard before, let alone tried before, and maybe a couple you've have heard before but you haven't had them taught to you from me personally.

Before we jump in, I want to make sure that you really acknowledge yourself. It's really important that you realize you're loving yourself, you're approving yourself, you're improving yourself by what you're doing here. Continue on with this. This is only step three. We're only at the halfway point so we have more lessons to do, more fun to have, more energy to expand, and more consciousness to widen.

What If I Don't Love Myself?

I know in previous lessons, people have asked, "What do I do if I don't love myself or I don't approve of myself or I don't like myself?" This is where it all changes. When you start to realize you're doing something for you, because of that, you're proving to yourself that you love yourself. You're proving that you care about yourself. You're proving that you are approving of yourself and you're improving yourself as you're doing all of this. So pat yourself on the back. Put your hand over your heart even and say, "I love you. I love you. I love you." That's where it all starts.

Common Questions

Before we go too far into this, I want to address some of the questions people have previously posed to me at this point in the process.

When I was born, my dad said 'She's ugly.' My mom said 'She is not a boy.' My sister nearly killed me with a blow as I came out of the hospital. I feel this and other issues have affected me all my life. How do you clear not just your own counterintentions but harmful intentions of others towards you?

The thing to realize is that counterintentions are not the other person's intentions—they are yours. The words and action may have come from the other people, but you're the one who accepted it at that point in time.

Now forgive yourself. You were not responsible for what they said to you when you were a baby. You weren't aware enough or conscious enough to know what was going on, let alone to know how to battle it or dismiss it or laugh it off. At that point in time, you're just downloading the information. We all went through a similar thing because we didn't have control over what was being said to us and about us.

The good news is because they are now your beliefs, you can erase them. You don't have to go to your sister or your brother or your dad or anybody and say, "Hey, take back what you said." They said what they said in the moment and they may have been doing the best they could based on their own limited belief system at the time. At this point, we want to forgive them. We want to let go of that memory and we want to work on the beliefs that we've taken on and brought to this moment.

It's good that you know what those beliefs are but it's even better to know that you can change them without going to anybody else. You don't need their permission. You don't need to change their minds. You don't need them to rewrite history. You can do that for yourself.

We're going to do that in this chapter. In these different processes that we're doing in this powerful session, you're going to be able to realize how you can change that in yourself because it's in you. It's not in them. *It's in you.*

Because it's in you and because you're doing these six steps, you'll be able to take care of this yourself. That's the great news. That's the freedom that you have now because as an awakening person, you're learning to take back your own power. You're learning to rewire your own brain. You're learning that you can take care of these beliefs that you've inherited without having to go to the people who passed them your way.

By clearing a counterintention, can I induce a change in my current circumstances or can I only see in myself a positive disposition to act and to follow inspiration, even when the circumstances remain the same?

That's a brilliant question because here's what happens when you change your intentions: When you change your belief, your entire life changes. Imagine the dominos. You know how when we were kids you probably saw somebody stack up those dominos in a line, close together but not right beside each other? Then somebody taps the first domino and all the dominos fall down. There are actually people who set up dominos all around the room and out into the street, and they tap that first domino, and all the dominos fall down all around the room and out into the street. They all fall.

That's what happens when you change a belief. When you change a belief—whether you know what it is or not—and you manage to get in and cleanse the unconscious mind to get rid of the counterintentions, your entire life actually changes. The beliefs that were there all rearrange themselves and your outer circumstances rearrange themselves to match the new belief. Actually, this is so powerful that when you change a core belief, a belief that's been with you your entire life and you change it now, and I mean *really* change it where it's no longer there, you will actually forget you ever had it.

It will almost be like a story you read in a book by somebody else but it didn't have anything to do with you. Or if you remember it, it will have no emotion on it. So it will change your history. It'll change your past. It'll change your present and it'll change your future timeline—that's how powerful it is. You certainly changed what was going on at that precise moment when you changed a belief, but you also alter the past and alter the future when you change the belief in this moment. Is that exciting or what?

This is one of the joyous things I get most enthused about because this is how we change our lives permanently and forever. What bothered us before is gone because we changed the belief now. And obviously you get to see what the new opportunities are and the new choices for the next moment, so it's the domino effect. All the dominos change when you change the core belief.

How important is it to be aware of your hidden beliefs? Can one do it on his/her own or is help from another necessary? Also, can't you clear those beliefs on a subconscious level without knowing exactly what you're clearing, just by meditating and doing the whole Ho'oponopono technique for example?

You do not need to know what the beliefs are. The questioner is absolutely right here. You don't need to know the beliefs. This is the wonderful thing.

If you do know what the limiting beliefs are, fine. Now you know what the target is. And you can actually aim to go for that particular belief and delete or change or get rid of that particular belief, but you don't need to know what it is.

Ho'oponopono is something I'm going to talk about later. In a future lesson, I'm going to give you the advanced technique on Ho'oponopono when I teach you how to activate Ho'oponopono, so it'll do even deeper work for you. But if you don't know what Ho'oponopono is, it's a Hawaiian healing system that's based on four phrases. I will share those phrases and we'll do a little bit of a Ho'oponopono cleansing later in this book. Then in the next lesson, step four, we'll go into this even deeper. You're going to love it. Most people, even if they've heard of Ho'oponopono before, haven't heard about the deeper activating aspects of it.

I wrote two books about it: *Zero Limits*, most people know about; and *At Zero*, written ten years later as a sequel to explain how I had learned about Ho'oponopono in the ten years that I had been practicing it. So there's a lot for me to share with you, but the important thing to know whether you know about Ho'oponopono or not, is you do not need to know the limiting beliefs. All you need to know is that you have a sense of a block. You have some sort of a recurring issue or challenge. You're not sure where it's coming from. You're not sure what the belief is but as long as you have that feeling—that's like an energy field in your body—you don't need to name the belief. Again, if you can that's great. That helps. But you don't need to.

Is there a way to get rid of all of those counterintentions in just one session? I do feel exasperated at times. I have been using the Ho'oponopono technique for a few years. I've used EFT, which is the tapping technique, and other techniques, and I am still working like a slave.

Well here's the key: you say, "I feel exasperated at times."

Please hear this. That is the clue to what really needs worked on. It isn't a matter of trying to find the one technique that removes everything out of your life in one session. It's like everybody's looking for the magic pill. "Tell me what pill to take and I'll take the pill and then I'll have limitless thinking and I'll be able to transform my life and all the negative beliefs will be deleted." It doesn't seem to work like that. That's why we have different techniques to help us get through this, and it is wonderful that that happens because this makes life joyous. This makes life fun. This makes life a game.

We get to find what the negative challenging beliefs are and delete them but notice something. When you talk about your beliefs, notice what kind of feeling you have when you think about them. Now the one who posed this question may or may not have been aware that when the question came up and he or she made the statement, "I feel exasperated." *Exasperated* is the *feeling* you want to delete. Exasperated is the feeling that's blocking your miracle from happening.

So, when you do Ho'oponopono, you do it on "exasperation" in your case. If you do EFT (Emotional

Freedom Technique) or TFT, which is the Thought Field Therapy, the tapping process that I told you about in the last chapter, you focus on "exasperation," because that was the key in your question. Are you with me?

You need to pay attention to your own language to understand this is how it's working. You are revealing your own limiting beliefs and you may not even know it unless you pay close attention.

All of these questions are great and I am very grateful for all the people who have asked them. I hope they have been helpful to you.

Watch What You Think

In this session we are going to go a little bit deeper, into counterintention clearing. We've already started, obviously, because one of the ways to clear negativity is with awareness, and by answering common questions of others who have worked through this, I'm trying to make you aware of how you think. I want you to become acutely sensitive to the thoughts going through your head, because as I've said in the last few lessons, you have 60,000 to 80,000 thoughts a day, and most of them are the same thoughts.

Have you done your homework and thought about what the recurring thoughts are in your life? Do you keep thinking that *I'm always exasperated*? Do you keep thinking that *I'm always ugly because I was told I was as a child*? Do you keep thinking that *it'll never work for me because it's never worked for me before*? Do you keep thinking that *all the good ones are taken so I'll never find the right match*? If those or something like them are your recurring thoughts, they hold the clue to what you want to delete and change. You want to be aware that you're actually reinforcing those negative thoughts as you keep thinking them. So you want to start to change your thoughts.

Now we're going to make it even easier to do so as we go through this lesson and the future ones, but I can't stress enough how important it is to be sensitive to your own thoughts. And as I said before, remember you are not your thoughts. You are separate from your thoughts.

In the future lessons, I'm going to go into this really deep and I'm going to have you discover and become one with your spiritual self, which will anchor in your life the way of walking miracles. The way of not only expecting miracles but walking miracles, creating miracles, manifesting miracles, and attracting miracles because you become one with the power source of spirit in you.

Using Meditation to Guard Your Thoughts

It's really important to pay attention to how you think. This is why meditation is really important. When you sit down to mediate, no matter what kind of meditation you do, your brain is still working. Your mind is still bubbling up ideas. And what you want to do is pay attention to those thoughts. What are the recurring thoughts? Are they all limited thinking? Are they all negative beliefs? Because *you can* change them. The very first step is awareness and that's my reminder for you right now.

Belief Busting

Belief busting is how we identify and remove bad beliefs. What I want you to do—and this is a very powerful process—is to start questioning your beliefs. You see, most of us take our beliefs as facts. The number one way to identify a belief is to ask yourself, "Is it true? Is it measureable? It is something we can all agree on?"

For example, if you're trying to attract a relationship and you, like so many people, think *all the good people are taken*. You can't find the love of your life because all of the good ones are taken. You may not know that's a belief. So you have to question it and say, "Is it true that all of the good people are taken?" When you realize that there are seven billion people on the planet—seven billion people—surely not all the good ones are taken! So the fact of the matter is, with seven billion people, the odds are stacked in your favor that you can find the good one for you.

By questioning *is it a belief* or *is it a fact*, you start to identify which ones aren't serving you. For example, a lot of people still think money is bad and a lot of that comes from the often-misquoted biblical scripture that says, "Money is the root of all..."—you just said evil, right? Is that a fact? Is money the root of all evil? Look at Mother Teresa; Mother Teresa used money. She collected money. People gave her money and she used it for good. Was money evil in that case? No. So it must not be the money, it must be the *belief* about money. You see what I'm doing here?

And say, for example, you're trying to change your health and maybe you're trying to gain weight or lose weight or overcome asthma or any number of things. You might be saying to yourself, "This is a lifelong struggle for me." Does that sound like a belief or a fact? It's a belief because you're giving your subjective interpretation to your life experience. Are there people around us in the world (with seven billion people on the planet) who have gained weight, lost weight, healed asthma, healed cancer, and overcome all kinds of health odds? I don't even care what it is. Name anything and somebody's overcome it. There are case studies of people who have overcome improbable, incurable, and impossible health situations. So if you say it's a lifelong issue for you, it's a belief, not a fact.

By separating the belief from the fact, you weaken the belief. This is really important. You weaken it just enough to start to believe, *wow, maybe it's possible for me to change.* That's a belief too, but it's a serving belief. It serves you better than any of the other beliefs that you were entertaining.

Belief versus Fact

You want to become aware of what you're telling yourself. You want to become aware of whether it's a belief or a fact. A fact is something on which we can pull out a ruler and measure. We can gather an entire room of people and ask them to tell us if they agree, and if everybody in the room agrees, and there're five hundred people there, it might be a fact.

But most likely, what you're telling yourself are beliefs. Beliefs about what you think are possible. Beliefs about yourself. Beliefs about your weaknesses, beliefs about your strengths, or beliefs about what you can do to change in life. You want to realize they're beliefs, and as long as they're beliefs, you can change them.

Pay attention to what you're thinking so you can hone in on the beliefs, because we want to bust the beliefs. Again, I'm here for you. I want you to have, do, or be whatever it is that you imagine. I want you to not only *expect miracles* but to *live miracles*. That's why I'm sharing this with you through this book. And that's why I'm so proud of you for being here with me, so we can do this together.

Set Your Intention for This Lesson

What I want you to do next is to remind yourself of what your goal is. What's the intention? In the very first lesson, I asked you to state something you wanted to have, do, or be. Then in the next lesson, I asked you to remind yourself of it, and I also said it might have changed. You might have refined it. Maybe you even completed it. Maybe you got what you wanted to have, do, or be and now it's time for you to focus on another item, another intention of some sort.

So, what's your intention for this lesson? You can use the same intention from the first or second class, or you can change it. This is your opportunity. Take a few seconds and just determine for yourself what do you intend? What do you want to have, do, or be? Do that over the next three seconds.

Okay, excellent. Now you might also write it down. Writing things down is always a good process; it'll help you anchor your intention. It tells your mind what you want, and it is also visible. You can see it and refer back to it. While thinking about your intention, ask what's in the way of you achieving it. Why hasn't it happened yet? What comes to mind for you? Now that's a rhetorical question. You don't need to answer it to me, but answer it for yourself because now we're going to go a little bit deeper.

Bust Your Own Beliefs

So you have an intention and now I've asked you to consider what's in the way. What's blocking the intention? Clearly ask yourself in an honest way: *why haven't I had the intention come to pass so far?* Write down your answer because your answer is revealing. Your answer is probably a belief.

You may say something like, "It's never going to happen for me. I don't have the money. I don't have the education. I don't have the experience. I don't have the connections. It's not in my DNA. I don't have the resources to do it. The astrological chart says that that's not going to happen in my lifetime."

There're all kinds of things that you're going to say. I want you to do what we were just talking about and ask yourself, "Is it a belief or is it a fact?" *Is it a belief or is it a fact?*

Your Turn: Role Play a Lunch with Joe

As you think about this, let's go deeper. One of the exercises that I advise people to do is what I'm advising you to do now and it is to notice how you talk about the events in your life. For example, you are going to have lunch with me tomorrow and we're going to have coffee and a salad.

We're going to talk about *The Miracle* book and I'm going to say, "Okay, did you get your intention?"

And you'll say, "No, I haven't gotten it yet," or maybe you'll say you did and we'll just celebrate.

But for the sake of this exercise, we'll say you said no, you didn't get the intention, and I'll ask, "Why didn't you get it? Why do you think it hasn't happened yet?"

And then you're going to give me an explanation. You're going to say something like, "Well, I tried five things last week and I tried two other classes and none of this stuff seems to work for me."

Then I'll stop and say, "Wait a minute. Is that a belief or a fact, because this stuff works for a lot of people? Earlier I told you about a woman who won forty million dollars in the lotto using visualization techniques and a lot of techniques that I've written about, and I think she even mentioned my book, *The Attractor Factor*, as one of her resources.

"And there're tens of thousands of people who have read my book and done my work or have been in my Miracles Coaching® program who have all kinds of stories of making change. So we know the techniques work. We know the processes work."

And so over our lunch and our coffee and salad, you say, "Well, I don't think they work for me."

I would say, "I think that's a belief. You telling yourself 'the processes won't work for me' is a belief, not a fact, because the processes have worked for virtually everybody who tries them. And when they don't work, it's because of a statement like that. *They don't work for me.* That's a belief. What you want to do is become aware of it. This technique is all about paying attention to how you describe events in your life."

Make it Real

What I invite you to do tomorrow is have coffee or lunch or dinner or an after work drink—whatever you like to do—with a friend and talk to them about something you're trying to manifest in your life. Tell them about some miracle that you would like to attract. And as you talk to them, pay attention to how you describe your reasons for not attracting it yet. Because you might say something like "Well, I'm going through a divorce and my spouse is really a Scorpion and you know once a Scorpion always a Scorpion. That person is never going to change."

Is that a belief or a fact? We know people change. So what you said is a belief, and as long as you have that belief, that the person is not going to change. You will be fueling it and it will be operating in your life.

Those are the kinds of beliefs we want to become aware of. And I can pretty much guarantee virtually everybody reading these words, including you, do not pay attention to how they explain their lives. They think that they're giving their rational, logical explanation for why things aren't working; not realizing what they're really giving is their belief system for why things aren't working. Are you with me? It's your belief system and that's what we're taking care of here.

Try It for Seven Days

The process above is what I want you to work on over the next seven days. When I say work, this isn't grueling work, this isn't sweat work, and this isn't labor. This is like being a detective. Just play with this. Just have a nice lunch or a nice drink with somebody and tell him or her your story over something you're trying to manifest. Give them your reasons for not manifesting it, and pay attention to yourself, because the reasons you're giving are the beliefs that are doing the attracting.

One way to look at this is the explanation that you give for an event is the belief that attracted the event. I'm pausing to let that sink in. *The explanation you give for an event is the belief that attracted the event.* That's a million dollar insight. Write that down, keep that with you, and do this particular process.

Counterintentions with Money

All that we're talking about are counterintentions and how to clear them. Again, clearing them can be as easy as being aware of them. When you become aware of your statements that, "Oh I thought money was evil," and you start to question, "Is money really evil? Can it be used for good? Maybe money is just neutral. Maybe it's just paper. Maybe money is nothing." (Pull out a dollar bill if you have one handy.) It's just a dollar bill. It's paper and ink.

We project emotion and meaning and symbolism onto this, but the dollar and this printed book are paper. One is significant only because I wrote words in it. The other paper is significant because the government printed it and they say it's worth a hundred pennies. But is there any inherited energy? Is this book evil? Is this money evil? No. They are neutral and this is the kind of thinking that will help you clear the counterintentions that you may not have been aware of.

Again, let's make this even juicer. We're going to go through some advance techniques to clear counterintentions. Are you excited or what? Because I am!

Socratic Questioning

What we're going to cover next are some techniques that I've come to use in the couple of decades that I've been doing this. One of the very first ones that I do is called *Socratic Questioning*. Socratic Questioning is so important to my life that at one point, thirty years ago, I printed up business cards. I actually found some fairly recently that said I was a Socratic Dialogue Consultant. Socratic Dialogue Consultant. That was thirty years ago. That's how long I've been doing this. Socratic Questioning is a way to question beliefs to realize that they are beliefs and not facts.

Identify a Belief

Let me invite you to do this as an example. To begin, I ask that you pick a known belief that's recurring in your life. What we want to do is question the belief. I will choose a common belief that others have like, "I am not as good as other people."

I am not as good as other people. I am going to use this as an example, but you can use whatever came up in your mind as the seed to work this particular technique.

I am not as good as other people is the *belief*. Now, first of all, we know that's a belief because there're certainly people out there that are (in very judgmental terms) *less than*, and some *more than*. All of us are the same. All of us are equal. All of us are beings of life. All of us are born of love. All of us are loving and lovable, but we're talking about *beliefs* and beliefs can make us very judgmental about ourselves.

Ask Yourself: Do You Believe That?

From a Socratic Questioning point of view, I would ask, "Do you believe that?" Do you believe, "I am not as good as other people"?

And what you're doing is questioning your belief with a very blatant question: do you believe your belief? Surprisingly, you may say, "No, I don't really believe the belief." You might actually say, "You know what? Now that I think about it, I don't believe that belief," and it's gone. It can be that easy.

But let's say it stays. Let's say you stated your belief, "I'm not good enough, I'm not good as other people, I can never find the right person. I can never get the body I want. I can never make the money I want. I can never be the success I want."

Take any belief and you ask yourself *do you believe it*? If you say "No," you're done. Belief is gone.

Why?

If you say, "Yes, I do believe it," ask the next question: "Why do I believe it?" Because what that question will do is unearth your own reasoning for your belief. What you're doing is playing detective. You're like an attorney. You're like Socrates, the great questioner, and you're questioning your own beliefs.

You can use this with whatever belief came to mind: *I'm not good enough. I'm not lovable. I'm not likeable.* You can use anything that comes to mind and ask, playing Socrates, "Do I believe it?" If you say, "Yeah, I do believe I'm not good enough." Why do you believe you're not good enough?

Then you'll come up with something like, "Well I heard it throughout my life and all the evidence around me says that I'm not good enough."

Dissect the Belief

Then you want to play Socrates and again ask *why do you believe you're not good enough, just because of that evidence?*

What you're doing is dissecting your belief. You are unwiring it. You're pulling it apart. You're dismantling it. You're playing Socrates. You're playing a good detective.

Continue to do this on your own. I advise you to do it with pen and paper and not just do it out loud. Write down, *I am not good enough*, and then write down, *do I believe I'm not good enough?* And you might write *no*, which is fine.

Or you might write *yes*. And if you write yes, write *why do I believe I'm not good enough?* Then whatever your answer is, write it down and question it. "Do I believe the evidence I just gave?" And you might say "No." And if you say, "Yes, I do believe the evidence I have for my belief," you want to ask, "Why? Why do I believe this evidence for that belief?" What you're doing is going through your own internal process of analyzing and dismantling your beliefs.

Come from Love

Now it's important to realize that Socrates or anybody that's doing this kind of Socratic Questioning does it from an unconditionally loving place, meaning that you're not judging your answers, and you're not judging yourself. You're accepting whatever comes in as the answer that's coming from your unconscious mind. You're trusting yourself. You're not judging yourself. You're not making yourself bad. You're not making yourself wrong. It's a spirit of unconditional love and absolute curiosity. That's what you want to have with the Socratic Questioning process.

Root Cause Erasing

Root cause erasing is really important. When you have a belief based on your experience that doesn't serve you well, you go to the root cause—the first time a belief was installed—and you "restory" it, you reframe it, you change everything in your life, like the domino effect, from that early point all through your life and onwards. It's a little bit like the movie *Back to the Future* when young Michael J. Fox goes back in time and he actually helps his father, who's a classmate back in time. Because the father made a new decision back in that primary root cause moment, the father changed all the way through that time period and became a different man when he came back to the future.

As an aside, this is ideal for the question that I addressed earlier: when she was born, her dad said, "She's ugly." Mom said, "She is not a boy." This is the exercise to do to address a situation like that. You can do this, depending on what comes up for you, because if you heard something like, "You'll always be alone" or

"You'll always be sickly" or "You are or she is ugly," you want to go to the first time you heard it.

The Process

This is how it works. To the best of your ability, you're using your mind to go back in time to the very first time you had that experience, because when you go to the first experience and you relive it and change it, it changes the belief forever and it changes you forever. In other words, when we were growing up, we were programmed by the people around us. They didn't do it intentionally. It wasn't like brainwashing. Our parents were probably not enlightened. My parents weren't enlightened.

They were downloading all of their beliefs about how the world works into your baby skull and by the time you were five, six, and seven years old, you were pretty hardwired personality-wise. It remains that way for most of your life until you get to a moment like this. And this moment becomes a turning point in your life because you can change all of it.

What I ask people to do for root cause erasing, is to actually remember as early as possible the first time you heard the belief. If the belief is *you're not good enough*, what's the first memory of that? Or if the belief is *I'm not as good as others*, what's the first memory of that? Or if the belief is *I've always had money problems* or

I've always had struggles with relationships, what's your first memory of that?

Take a few seconds to think about your own belief and first memory.

You have to let your brain bring up a memory. When it does, it may be fairly recent. That's okay because that fundamental early belief is the one attracting all those stories and all those experiences you've had in the past.

We want to go back even further. How much further back can you go in memory? Can you go all the way back to being a teenager? Can you go back to being in grade school? How far back can you go? What is the first or earliest memory you have of hearing that belief? Take what your memory is giving you. Don't judge it. It's not right, wrong, or indifferent. It's just the memory that's coming up and it's perfect for this moment and for this process.

Now, relive it in your mind. Just see it happening in your mind. And close your eyes for a second and you could see that you're five years old or seven years old or twelve, whatever it is, and you relive the moment and imagine—let it play. And imagine now that you've stopped and asked yourself how old you were when that took place. Maybe you were five. Maybe you were ten years old. Maybe you were twelve years old.

Then ask yourself what kind of awareness you had about beliefs, about life, and about yourself at that point in time. Truth is, hardly any. You weren't mature enough. You weren't aware enough. You weren't conscious enough to be able to make any judgment call on what you were hearing at that time. So you made a conclusion about how life works, based on the experiences of a five-year-old or a ten-year-old or a twelve-year-old. That should be pretty freeing in itself.

And then what we want to do is ask, "What else could it have meant?" Now play with this for a little bit. Even with the questioner who was called ugly, and the things they heard from their father and mother, maybe just for the sake of the exercise, maybe they were joking. Maybe they were kidding. Maybe it was their own personal belief system and their own personal disappointment, which had nothing to do with that person. Just consider the source for a minute. Then ask, what it could have meant or what you want it to mean.

Root Cause Erasing Recap

1. Go back to the earliest experience of the belief
2. Relive it and identify your conclusion (the belief you held since then)
3. Ask yourself what age, mentality, and awareness you were at that time (realize you made a conclusion based on an uneducated life experience)
4. Ask yourself "What else could it have meant?" (Make up anything)
5. Finally, ask what you want that first experience to mean

An Example from My Life

In my case, my parents struggled with money. When I was growing up, the worst arguments I heard were over money. Remember, I went through poverty. I went through homelessness. I lived out their beliefs, because I felt money was evil and money was a struggle; I lived it out of my belief system and it seemed real to me. It seemed factual to me until I did the root cause erasing. Then I got to the point where I realized that those beliefs were my parents'. The beliefs weren't mine.

My parents had beliefs about money. I took them on when I was a child because I didn't know any better. When I became an adult and started doing work on myself like root cause erasing, I got to the point where I realized I could change it. What I realized was it was *their* belief and they are welcome to have their beliefs until they're ready to change their beliefs, but I chose to change the belief.

I changed that core belief in that early memory, as an adult, by going back in time, which is what I'm advising you to do. Go back in time to the first experience and then restore it. Reframe it. Find a new belief for it. Write down or say to yourself, "It was their belief. That was their limited thinking. It had nothing to do with me. I'm a child of God. I'm a child of the universe. I'm a child of nature. I'm a child of love. I'm a child of miracles." And with that new belief, I took on a whole different life and you will too. That's *root cause erasing*.

What's Your Belief?

People have sent me all kinds of belief statements. "Being beautiful is dangerous." Obviously that's a belief. You want to question it. "Being totally blind is very difficult." That's an interesting one because being totally blind is very difficult. I'm sure it is, and yet that's a belief because the fact is, there are hundreds of thousands of people who have cured blindness and have actually lived with blindness in a joyous way. And I speak from personal experience. I'm not making this up. This is why it's so important to find the difference between beliefs and facts.

If you just live with the belief that blindness is a struggle or it's difficult (I'm sure everybody would agree it is), it's a limitation. If you look at it as a belief that can be changed, now you're empowered.

For example, way back in the 1980s, I was writing articles for feature magazines. I wrote a cover story about Meir Schneider. Meir Schneider was born blind in Israel. He was *born* blind. He has a certificate that says he is blind, but today he can read it to you. He drives a car. He lives in San Francisco [CA, USA]. He has written books about overcoming blindness. He teaches blind people how to see and I have interviewed him. I have met him and I put on a seminar years ago in San Diego [CA, USA] and I had him as one of my featured speakers. He is still helping people to overcome blindness, to find the joy in it, and to actually be okay with it.

This is what I mean about all of these different beliefs that we throw out. We think it's the end. We think it's a fact. We think it's unchangeable, where in the *expect miracles* prospective of the world, the one I'm giving you and teaching you and helping you with, anything is possible. Nothing is impossible. You can have, do, or be anything you want.

Is it Impossible to be Wealthy?

Somebody actually wrote me to say, "I believe it's impossible to be wealthy." Obviously that's a belief and they can question it. They can do the *Socratic Questioning*.

"Do you really believe it's impossible to be wealthy?"

They may say, "Yes."

And I'll say as a Socratic Questioner, "Why do you believe it's impossible for you to be wealthy?"

And then they'll give their answer and their answer is going to reveal more beliefs that they can question.

If this was your belief, you could also do the *root cause erasing* and actually ask yourself "When was the very first time in my life that I heard that I might not ever be wealthy? How far back does that go?" And then see if you can find that root cause, the prime directive, that moment when it took place. Locate the defining moment when the belief was installed and go back and question the circumstances, question who was telling it to you, and question your memory (you don't have to actually question the other people).

And then reinterpret it and say, "Wait a minute. That was a belief from somebody else. They said I could never be wealthy or I concluded I could never be wealthy because of what I saw around me. Is that actually a fact?"

No. You can be wealthy. If I can go from poverty and homelessness to being wealthy, anybody can. I am not different. I am not special. And I'm not the only one. This is the kind of empowerment I'm trying to give to you.

Emotional Freedom Technique (EFT)

I talked about EFT or tapping in the last chapter, so I'll just mention it briefly here. EFT is the Emotional Freedom Technique and it's a way of tapping away the belief. For example, I can take one of the beliefs that people have shared with me, like, "All my wishes should not be granted." So you would take that belief and say, "Even though I believe all my wishes cannot be granted, I deeply love, accept, and forgive myself," using the tapping process I discussed in step two. This is the key phrase that I would say as I tap on the karate chop point at the bottom palm of my hand. You would insert whatever the key phrase is for you. Then tap through the other points.

Other key phrases might be: "Being beautiful is dangerous." "I have to work long, hard hours to earn a living." "I'm not attractive because I'm fat." "I believe it's impossible to become wealthy." "I do not believe in the abundance of the universe." These are all beliefs that others have shared with me that could be tapped away. Pick the one that fits you and use it as a phrase.

Remember, the Emotional Freedom Technique or Thought Field Therapy is promoted by Gary Craig, Nick Ortner, Roger Callahan, and others. You can find tapping videos online.

Ho'oponopono

Ho'oponopono is the Hawaiian healing technique I mentioned before. I'm going to give you the advanced and activated version of it in the next session. There I will go in depth into expanding your consciousness, taking apart the four stages of awakening, walking you through those stages, and also teaching you about Ho'oponopono.

There's a miraculous story about Ho'oponopono healing so many people, and after doing it for ten years, I have seen and heard from tens of thousands of people who are practicing Ho'oponopono.

The short version of it is basically four phrases. "I love you. I'm sorry. Please forgive me. Thank you." *I love you. I'm sorry. Please forgive me. Thank you.* And those four phrases, you say inside, to yourself, to your connection to Divinity, to God, to nature, to the higher power, to the great something, or whatever you want to call it. And you're asking as a kind of prayer to remove the lack, the limitations, the beliefs, and the counterintentions—whether you know them or not—within your data system and your unconscious mind.

You're basically thinking about what the block is, whether you can name it or not, and you're saying to yourself, "I love you. I'm sorry. Please forgive me. Thank you. I love you. I'm sorry. Please forgive me. Thank you." And you're doing that over and over to your connection to the Divine. You don't do it to another person. You're not saying it to another person. You're saying it to God, if you will. The Divine if you will. And you're asking the Divine to clean this up with those magic phrases.

Again, there's a lot to Ho'oponopono and you will love hearing the story, and hearing how to activate it, and learning more about it, which I will do in the next lesson and those that follow. You will love it. It's so easy.

I hear from celebrities who use Ho'oponopono. Very famous people, authors, leaders, singers, actors, actresses, people from all walks of life including the next door neighbors and they use it on everything. They use it for their pets. They use it for health. They use it for money. They use it for relationships. They use it for just about anything you can name.

So that's Ho'oponopono—those are the basic four phrases—and you can say them now and start to benefit. But we'll go into them deeper in the chapters to come.

Miracles Coaching®

Miracles Coaching® is another way to handle things. Miracles Coaching® is a whole separate process. That's where you actually work with a Miracles Coach; somebody trained in my methods to help you get clear.

In my life, I have found that there's nothing more powerful than having a Coach, somebody who's trained to listen to you and be objective with you and help you be accountable and help you go for your goals. Most great athletes have a coach. Many successful businesspeople have coaches. If you're interested in Miracles Coaching®, go to www.Miraclescoaching.com. I'm not trying to sell you anything. This is just for you to be aware of—it's a tool that I started many years ago and one I believe in.

Sending Positive Energy

I want to send a little energy to you. I'm sending some esoteric clearing to you. It's the Reiki energy; it's the Qigong energy. It's the metaphysical clearing energy, and I'm intending that this go to you. I'm also doing Ho'oponopono. I'm saying, "I love you, I'm sorry, please forgive me, thank you," inside myself as I'm thinking of you.

I'm doing all of this because this is a way for me to pray for you. Also, I do believe in angels and I think most of us have angels that are unemployed because we don't ask for any help from them. I've learned to speak out loud because I don't think my angels are mind readers; I've asked them to do something. Like before producing this chapter, I said, "Angels, please give the most benevolent outcome for me to help these people in the clearest, most loving, and most inspired way. Thank you. Thank you. Thank you. Thank you."

I invite you to do that too. Receive the energy. Do Ho'oponopono and don't be afraid to speak out loud and ask for help. (Do it alone, of course.) Do it as a kind of prayer ritual for yourself, but ask for the angels' help.

The Secret Prayer

I wrote a book called *The Secret Prayer*, and in the book, I said there's a **three-step formula** for praying. The **first step** is to be grateful now. I really feel that if you're grateful now, then everything else falls into place, because gratitude is the fundamental miracle. Be grateful now. Feel grateful. Look around and find something that you're grateful for.

The **second step** is to make a detached request. What I mean is, don't be addicted or don't be needy or don't be demanding in having things work out in a particular way. Make a detached request. For example, the first two steps could sound like: "I'm really grateful for my life," (that's step one) and "It'll be really cool if I had so and so," fill in the blank for what you'd like to have, do, or be (that's step two, the detached request).

The **third step** is to take inspired action, which I talk about a lot. That means when you have an idea for something or there's an opportunity in front of you, you leap on it because it's the inspired action. You seize it as a signal from the universe to fulfill your prayer request. So as a process, the secret prayer is gratitude, detached request, and inspired action.

Yagnas and Mantras

A mantra is simply a phrase that you say over and over again. There are many of them in the Sanskrit language. One that I like is called Gayatri. Look it up on Google because there're many forms of it. You can find it. It's only a paragraph and you might pray over it or use it as a kind of meditation.

Ho'oponopono is a mantra. "I love you. I'm sorry. Please forgive me. Thank you," is a mantra. You're saying that over and over again; it's a process.

Yagna is something you've probably never heard of but it's one of my secret allies. I have had a yagna done for me for each day of the last fifteen years. A yagna is an Indian ritual of cleansing. Five or more Indian priests/practitioners get together and chant and pray and do mantras on my behalf. You can have them do that for you as well. There is a fee for it. There's a donation of some sort and there're different services that use it. Now again, I'm not trying to sell you anything. I'm just giving you a tool that you may want to check out. One source that I know is Yagnas-By-Choice, which is online at www.yagnas-by-choice.com. There're other ones out there as well. This may not be of interest to you or you may find it to be something that is pretty timely and pretty powerful.

Choose What Works Best for You

I have covered several esoteric clearing methods, and of course, I'm sending you energy, even now, and I'm going to continue to do this as we round out this chapter.

We have covered a tremendous amount of material. I have given you a lot of content and a lot of processes, but this chapter, in particular, has had a flood of information. I want you to pick what really works for you and use it. You don't have to do everything (there's a lot here), but try a few things. It is like going to a buffet and choosing what you like best.

Common Questions

Let's address a few more questions that I am often asked after learning all of this material. You may have some of these same questions, or may just learn from the responses.

I am someone with serious procrastination issues. Are there any techniques for dealing with procrastination or the lack of discipline to practice these techniques and take inspired action?

The big thing here is to realize that there is a belief behind you not taking action. As an example, using the Socratic dialogue process, I would be sitting there and I would say, "Okay, so you've been procrastinating. Why do you think you procrastinate?"

And then you would give me an answer. Then we would explore that and I would say, "Okay, why do you believe that's keeping you from taking the action that you know that you want?"

In other words, there's some soul searching here. There's some belief work to be done here and that's for everybody that has a procrastination issue, because I hear that's one of the number one things people struggle with.

I've talked about it before, but I'm going to tell you that people procrastinate for only a couple of reasons and two are the fear of failure and the fear of success. They're afraid that they're actually going to be successful or they're afraid that they're actually going to fail. Both of those are beliefs. Both of those can be questioned. And when you question them and get free of them, then you realize like—*Well there's no reason not to take action. I'll just start doing it.* Those are the first two reasons: having a belief about failure or success.

Another reason people sometimes procrastinate is because what they want to do is bigger than what they think they can handle. It's just too gigantic of a project. I just tell them to break it down into bite-sized pieces, or baby steps, and do the very first baby step. That's what you want to do.

Look at procrastination from that aspect and really know that it's a form of self-sabotage. You're keeping yourself from your own good. You know you want to take action. You know you want to do the belief work. You know you want to have the results, but you're stopped from doing it. You want to look at what's stopping you. As you do, use any of the techniques we've been talking about in this chapter to address the belief. I know there're a lot of them here and I apologize if it's overwhelming, but pick the one or two that really seem to connect with you and work on that.

Also look at the fear of failure or the fear of success. Neither one are anything to be afraid of. I know from personal experience: I've failed and I've been a success. Neither one is anything to be afraid of, and once you know that, you'll be fine.

How do I build consistency?

That just comes over time. Take me for example: I've written fifty or more books and I recently signed a contract for another book, *The Awakened Millionaire,* that comes out in 2016. I have fifteen music albums, and more music will be coming out in the future. People ask me, "How in the world do you do this?" Well, I didn't set out thirty years ago to write fifty books. I set out to write one book, and after I wrote the one book, another book became apparent to me. I wrote that. But I still wasn't thinking about fifty books; I was doing one at a time. As you do one at a time, you build consistency.

Another way to approach consistency is to do good things for yourself every day. A fun technique is to pick five good things to do for yourself every day.

- One of them might be to go into a social media group and participate there. Help other people. Post your comments and let others know what you're doing. It's a good thing for you to do.
- Another good thing to do for yourself is to write an affirmation. Something you want to have, do, or be. *I now have the love of my life. I am now in my perfect body. I now have the ideal job.* Something like that.
- A third thing you might do is Nevillize a goal or something you want to have. Imagine you already have it. What does it feel like when it's already taken place? How does it feel now that it is already a part of your life experience?

- A fourth thing you might do is take a bubble bath. I get in a hot tub almost every night, in Texas, and I look at the wonderful sky and give thanks for it. I bathe myself. I nurture myself. I approve of and love myself.
- And a fifth thing you can do is spend some time feeling gratitude and writing five things you're grateful for.

You do what feels right for you. Create consistency by starting today and continuing tomorrow. As simple as that sounds, that's where it begins. You start today and continue tomorrow and continue the next day, and you'll have consistency over time.

You answered a previous question saying that there is no need to know what the belief is in order to clear it, and then later you spoke about root cause erasing. Can you please explain the difference?

That's a great, great question. You don't need to know the belief. You don't need to know it at all. What I said was you needed to know the overall feeling, and if you have the overall feeling, you can clear it. If you did have the belief, then certainly you can do the root cause erasing and ask yourself, "When did I first have that belief?" So if you know the belief, you can use that process and try to trace it back to the first memory—the first cause for the root cause belief.

If you don't know what the belief is, but you always have a feeling there when you're feeling blocked, you can use that feeling. Perhaps it's a feeling of frustration. It's a feeling of exasperation. It's a feeling of desperation. It's a feeling of unhappiness. So you use that feeling and you ask a question such as, "When was the first time I felt exasperated? When was the first time I felt unhappy? When was the first time I felt (whatever the feeling is)?" Do you see what I'm saying? You don't need to know the belief, but you do need to know either the belief or the feeling to help trace it to its root. I am grateful for the question to help clarify that.

Celebrate Your Success

Before we wrap up this important chapter, I want to mention a couple of things. I want you to realize that you're doing fantastic. This may be confusing at times and perhaps even overwhelming, but you're going through a process of awakening, and in three lessons, you have done a lot of work and covered a lot of content and processes.

In the next chapter it's going to become clearer as I talk about Albert Einstein. He had that famous quote that basically said that you can't solve your problems on the same level of consciousness that created them. Now stop and think about that. That's a powerful quote but he's also implying that you have to leave the consciousness you're in to change or get rid of your problem. And that leads to the challenge: how do you change your consciousness? If you're in your consciousness, the very consciousness that's creating the problem, how do you leave your consciousness to not have that problem?

So far we have been expanding your consciousness; in the next lesson I'm going to really take this apart and it will really delight you, educate you, and entertain you. We'll talk about the four stages of awakening. In later chapters, we're going to talk about the advanced/activated form of Ho'oponopono. I'm going to talk about responsibility and how to turn beliefs inside out and so much more. I'm very excited because that's really a turning point.

We're going deeper into all of this and as you actually expand your consciousness and become more awakened and grow even more, you learn that life really is one of miracles. And you can *expect miracles* as you begin to *live miracles*.

The Hook

I'd like to end this chapter with the lyrics to a song called "The Hook." It's an original song from my album called *One More Day: Life Lessons in Hypnotic Song* performed by me with my band. "The Hook" is a song that reminds you not to take the hooks that either your mind gives you or other people give you. You know what I'm talking about.

You're driving in traffic and all of a sudden, somebody pulls out in front of you and you get mad. You just took the hook. Or maybe you go to work one day and somebody mumbles something under his or her breath and it pushes a button in you. You took the hook. Or maybe you're meditating and a thought comes into your mind about something somebody said three weeks ago or three years ago and suddenly you're upset. You took the hook. So the song is a reminder: don't take the hook.

You are not a victim to your thinking. I want you to be a victor. That's what all of this is about—to awaken so you can have, do, and be what you want, and so you can expect miracles and attract, have, and live miracles.

So the song printed on the next page is called, "Don't Take the Hook." (We just call it "The Hook" for short.) It's my reminder to you that I want you to *expect miracles* because anything is possible. You can gain access to the song online at www.AllHealingMusic.com. It is available on iTunes and CDBaby.

I will be back with you in the next chapter: *Einstein's Secret*.

THE HOOK

WORDS AND MUSIC ©2015 BY JOE VITALE. ALL RIGHTS RESERVED.
WWW.ALLHEALINGMUSIC.COM

don't take the hook
it'll steal your mind
it's a horrible crime
don't take the hook

don't take the hook
let the moment go
be still and know
don't take the hook

> don't take the hook
> don't bite the bait
> livin' free and easy
> is really great

don't take the hook
turn the other cheek
smile at the weak
don't take the hook

don't take the hook
your peace is here
all is well my dear
don't take the hook

> don't take the hook
> don't bite the bait
> livin' free and easy
> is really great

don't take the hook
someone says something mean
you want to scream
don't take the hook

> don't take the hook
> don't bite the bait
> livin' free and easy
> is really great

STEP FOUR

Einstein's Secret

To be transformed, the whole basis of your thoughts must change. But your thoughts cannot change unless you have new ideas, for you think from your ideas.

—Neville Goddard

I'm very excited because we have reached a turning point. We've got two more chapters after this: five and six. But this is a turning point because this is where we're going to really go deep into some information that you really need to know.

You've already done three lessons, so congratulate yourself. Three lessons, three chapters, and a lot of material has been covered. There have been a lot of insights, a lot of techniques, a lot of processes, and we're still moving along.

Ho'oponopono Invocation

To ensure we are on the same page, I want to read a Ho'oponopono invocation that is at the front of my book *At Zero*. It is very simple, but just treat it like a cleansing prayer because I am cleansing myself so I can be here for you, but I'm also cleansing you so you can be here for me. This way we are on the same moment and we are connected.

> *O infinite divine mind. Through my beloved high self, cleanse this unit of all negativity both within and without so that it may be a perfect vessel for your presence. I love you. I'm sorry. Please forgive me and thank you.*

Consciousness Expansion

This chapter is called *Einstein's Secret* because at this point in the book, we want to expand our minds. The rest of these lessons are all about bringing you to a state of awakening. In that state of awakening is where you will experience miracles. You no longer even *expect miracles*, you actually *live miracles*.

Einstein said, *"We can't solve problems by using the same kind of thinking we used when we created them."*

That's a powerful insight. What he's really saying is that if we keep wrestling with life and our challenges and our problems with the same mindset, with the same belief system that actually created all of the problems, then we are not going to resolve the problems. We will probably create other problems and other challenges and never break free...never break out...never break through, and what I want you to do is break through.

I want you to break through the lower levels of consciousness and reach higher levels. I'm going to go through the four stages of awakening, although you already know a couple of them. However, we're going to go through those two briefly and then address the other two so that you'll really have some ground work on where I'm taking you over this lesson and the following two.

This is very exciting because there's never been a process like this. What you're learning in this book is leading edge material. You've both invested in yourself and you've begun to transform yourself one lesson at a time, one step at a time, and that's how life works. One moment at a time, we create miracles.

Managing Ourselves Among Others

Someone once shared with me that she was watching her thoughts and trying to remain separate from them, but she didn't know how to manage being bothered by the actions of others. She asked my advice for how to avoid attitudes in others or what she could do to change what others were doing.

I shared with her that what we're talking about here is not changing other people. We're not in this to change other people. This is not a course in persuasion. It's not a course in influence. It is a process for changing *you*. And this is really important to get because somebody else might give you a pat answer on how to handle the other people that might be bothering you. It's not about other people.

The way I'm teaching this—and the way Einstein is actually directing us—is to go past the level of consciousness that actually perceives this as a problem. We want to go past it and realize everything we see in the world is actually a projection from inside of us. The work we have to do is inside ourselves, not in other people, not with other people, not for other people, not about other people.

In Ho'oponopono, the Hawaiian healing system that Dr. Hew Len taught me, they say that there are no other people. They don't actually exist except as a figment of your imagination. Now, I know when you see these people, they seem real to you, but what you have to realize as we go into these greater stages of awakening and we get to the point we actually create miracles is that they—the people you see on the outside—are reflections of you. *They're reflections of what's in you.* What's bothering them—what's bothering you about them—is actually what's *in you* that bothers you about yourself.

Now this is a huge concept so you may not get it right at this moment, but please trust me and sit with this for a spell. Let me tell you a funny story that illustrates this. This is an analogy.

What's Wrong with Everybody?

I recently went to a concert, and when we left, it was late at night. We stopped and had dinner, then I valet parked my car, and finally, we went to a guitar concert. Afterwards, we got back in the car and we drove home. As we're driving home, I noticed that *boy, people are pulling out in front of me and why are they doing that on the road?*

There were some bicyclists and I could barely see them and I thought *why don't they have better lighting on their bikes?* I noticed, as I was driving, that the traffic seemed to be unusually crazy. I drove forty miles for forty minutes and then I heard sirens and saw the flashing lights in the rear view mirror. I was pulled over by a policeman. I didn't know what I was doing wrong because I wasn't speeding. I was in a nice car; all the inspections, legalities, and everything were fine. But, he pulled me over and I rolled down my window as he walked up.

"That's a really beautiful car to be driving without any headlights," he said.

I immediately went, "What? No headlights? The headlights on my car come on automatically. It's a new car. It's a very nice car. I don't have to touch the headlights. It senses when it's dark and the headlights come on."

What I soon realized was that somebody at valet parking turned that switch off. When I got in the car and started it up, the headlights didn't come on. The running lights on the car may have engaged, hence being enough light for me to get by.

I realized then that all of those people I had complained about hadn't done anything wrong. The bicyclist didn't need more light. *I needed my headlights.* Those people who pulled out in front of me in traffic didn't need to have more lights or to do anything differently; after all, they couldn't see me because I didn't have my headlights on.

This turned out to be a humorous metaphor showing that *it's not about the other people, it's about you.* What this book teaches you is that the more you work on yourself, the more you clean yourself and clear yourself and get to these greater stages of consciousness and awakening, those people will then follow suit by changing. You must realize, however, that this is not because of anything you did to them, but what you did to yourself on the inside.

Another way to look at this is this: by now everybody knows the story about Dr. Hew Len, the therapist who taught me Ho'oponopono because I wrote the first book *Zero Limits* about it, and then I wrote the second book *At Zero* about it. But to reiterate for a moment, Dr. Len worked at a hospital for the mentally insane, and he helped heal all of the hospital's mentally insane criminals. However, if you remember the story correctly, he didn't actually work with them. He didn't try to change them. He changed himself.

As he changed himself, they healed. Can you see the difference? It's really not about trying to change your family, friends, or anybody. It's really about changing you, and this will become clearer as you grow.

The Fear of Change

Change can be scary sometimes. Several people who have worked through the processes we have covered still seem to have a constant, lingering fear that they can't quite identify. The question is: Is it really necessary to know what the fear is, or can they remove it by using the techniques we've talked about?"

I love this question because the answer is so simple. No, you do not need to know what the fear is. At the same time, if you do know what the fear is, if you can put a label on it and if you could find a belief behind it, that's fine. But, either way, you either know the *belief* or you know the *feeling* and either one of them can be healed. *If you can feel it, you can heal it.* If you're feeling a fear, that's wonderful because you know that there is some sort of thought form that you're calling a fear and what you want to do is release it. You want to love it, you want to appreciate it, and you want to know it's there to protect you.

This brings up a good point, which is that a lot of us are afraid of fear. It sounds ironic, but we're afraid of fear because we think it's harmful, and yet the truth is, fear is to protect you. Much like the previous question, what you're doing is realizing that on some level you're afraid of change and so you're fearful. You fear that *if I change, how will my life be? How will I be different?* And what you want to realize is how your life will be is fantastic and how you will be is happy and healthy and miraculous and living in a state of moment by moment awe.

So when you realize the fear is actually a good thing and the fear is trying to protect you and then you go deeper and realize that there is nothing to actually protect you from, that all of this material—and even this process—is designed to be *good for you* and *to help you*, then you can let the fear go. To simply answer this question, you don't need to know or name the fear beyond the notion that it exists.

Your Turn: Success Stories

One thing that can help us to change our consciousness as Einstein suggests, is to recognize what is working in our lives. Seeing our own successes can move us from victimhood to empowerment. To that end, take a moment to do this exercise.

In one or two lines, write down something good that you manifested since you have been reading this book and working through the steps. *Did you manifest something? Did you attract something? Did you accomplish something?*

Was there something you were struggling with and you dissolved it? Write it down.

I want to point out something using a horseshoe as an example. I took an authentic horseshoe that was made out of metal and made for a horse, and I straightened it. I did what others might find impossible and I bent it.

I bent it with mind power.

I bent it with will power.

I bent it with muscle power.

I bent it with endurance.

I bent it with intention.

I bent it with commitment, but I bent it.

I'm sharing this with you because we can have, do, or be anything. I don't care what you think is impossible; I believe there's a way to achieve and attract anything. You may not know what the way is in this very moment; however, you can learn it, you can discover it, and you can create it.

Here are some examples of what other people have achieved through just the first few phases of this process:

- *I have a sister who always wanted a free reading and last week she actually went and booked and paid for it.* Sounds great.
- *I was able to dissolve my obsession with an unhealthy relationship by learning that I am 100% responsible for attracting it.* All right.

- *I've figured out my root cause of my counterintentions. I've felt so insufficient and worthless for all of my life. Break through.* I loved hearing this!
- *I was accepted into the art showing I wanted to be in.* Awesome! Congratulations!
- *I have a relationship at a new level, an $8,000 raise, and several accepted publications.* All right, woo-hoo on that one!
- *I landed an interview at a local library, gained clarity about who I am, and have value where I can contribute.* All good things.
- *I manifested a repair from a place that apparently was closed.* Awesome.

These examples go on and on. And there are a lot more. I can't share all of these, but I wanted to give you to a sense of the accomplishments people have received from the processes in this book. The more you work with this material, the more successes you will be able to share. So keep writing them down.

Moving through the Stages of Awakening

You already know some of the four stages of awakening because I talked about **the first stage**, victimhood, already. Victimhood is one we all know really well. That's when we all feel like crap. We all feel like the world is stacked against us and we don't stand a chance and we're the walking dead. That's when we are constantly recreating the same problems again and again like Einstein said.

I want to make sure you know that most people are born into victimhood. Most people live by what Henry David Thoreau said, "We're living lives of quiet desperation." Inside, they're unhappy and unhealthy and they feel like a victim. That's the nature of victimhood. Most people are born into that. Most people grow up living that way. Most people die that way. Fortunately you're not there anymore. You've gone way beyond it because you're reading this book. You're already in lesson four. You've already left victimhood.

The second stage, which is so thrilling and we've talked a lot about that too, is empowerment. Empowerment is where you have the feeling that you can have, do, or be anything. It is an incredible feeling. It's a thrilling feeling. It's a powerful feeling. It's an energetic feeling.

When people are lucky enough to see a movie like *The Secret* or to read one of my books like *The Attractor Factor* or *Zero Limits* or to read books of the other people like Bob Proctor, Jack Canfield, or Lisa Nichols (there are many great teachers out there with a lot of great material), they can have one of the first awakenings in their life.

However, it's not the *only* awakening. That's why these *Six Steps to Enlightenment* include the four stages of awakening. People can have the first major awakening when they leave victimhood and move into empowerment. Empowerment is wonderful because now we have tools to use to make a difference in our lives. It's jubilant. Be grateful for that.

Empowerment is fantastic, and you already know some of that because with empowerment you can *visualize* your life. You can *affirm* your life. You can *Nevillize* your life. You can *script* your life. You can have *affirmations* for your life. You can do *The Remembering Process*. There are so many tools to help you when it comes to empowerment.

Empowerment is the second stage of awakening. As we move into the next stage, we're making it even more powerful because we have all these tools and now we're adding the Divine to our side.

The third stage is what I'm calling surrender. Surrender, for the most part, is the new one here in our lesson. Surrender doesn't mean giving up. A lot of people confuse the word surrender with just saying, "Well, I can't do anything. It is what it is." And they give up. That's not what I'm talking about here. Surrender, the way I'm talking about it as a third stage of awakening, is when you surrender to a higher power.

It is when you surrender to Divinity; surrender to God; surrender to nature. Surrender is when you realize your ego can't run the ship. Your ego can't drive the bus through life. Your ego can't see all the options and opportunities and choices you have available to you in any one moment. So your ego is very limited and you have to join forces with something else and that's where the Divine comes in. I can't find the words to describe how overwhelmingly powerful it is to join with the Divine as your ally to create what you want.

Now, I use the word Divine. You can use God. You can use miracles. You can use nature. You can use higher power. You can use the universe. You can use all there is. You can use the great something. All of these are words for what I'm calling Divinity.

Now, my wake up call for learning to surrender was because of Dr. Hew Len and Ho'oponopono and I wrote about that in the book *Zero Limits* and again in the follow-up book *At Zero*.

Let me give you some concrete examples. Several years ago, in Texas, we had wildfires and the wildfires were out of control. Hundreds of homes were burned to the ground. Thousands and thousands of acreage and forests were burnt. The fire was so big and so raging that man couldn't stop it. We didn't have enough water. We didn't have enough manpower. We didn't have enough helicopters dumping water on it to make a difference. I realized that if I really were in control of the world, I would put out those fires; I mean wouldn't you?

But I couldn't. I had to surrender. It didn't mean that I had no power because I still can do some things, and I'll talk about those a little later in this particular lesson, but I couldn't stop the fires.

The same thing happened in the town where I live a few months ago when we had a Biblical level flood. A little stream, which flows through the city, rose forty-six feet and became a tidal wave and demolished homes. Friends of mine lost their homes.

My webmaster and his wife and kids were sleeping upstairs when they heard water. They had to swim out of their house with their pets. The water enveloped their house to the point where they had to swim out! That was unusual. A lot of people went through that, so there was a lot of sudden suffering there.

If I were in control of everything, I would have stopped that flood. Wouldn't you? And I can go on with these kinds of stories, and you get to the point where you realize that you have to surrender to a higher power that knows more than you and has more energy, more wisdom, and more power than you personally do.

A lot of people run into this when there's a life threatening issue and they feel like they can't handle it by themselves. This is where they turn and say, "Somebody else has to help. I can't do it on my own."

Just three weeks ago, one of my best friends, one of my mentors, a person who's been dear in my life, died. He had been dying over a period of time, and I saw him before he died, but if I could have done anything to save him, I would have done it. So it's important to realize that the third stage is about awakening to a state of surrender by joining forces with a higher power, which you can call God, and at that point, you can allow Divinity to come through.

The good news, the great news is that when you allow that to happen, you can create by God, miracles, because God is helping you. They are by God. It is you and the Divine jointly working together to make these miracles happen. Then is when you can expect miracles in life because it's not just you trying to make a difference. It's you *and* the universe working together.

Miracle of Surrender: Working with the Divine

There are so many stories I can tell you. Let me share one that ought to hit home. Five or six years ago, it could have been longer, my mother was taken to the intensive care at the hospital and all of the family was called in. I canceled speaking engagements and travel plans. She was in an enclosed intensive care unit where there were only five other people in the same unit.

This was crucial care and three of the other five people passed away while I was there. And there was my mother...and I was sitting there going, *I know all these techniques, I know all these tools, but I can't help her.* So what I did was surrender. And I surrendered with Ho'oponopono.

I sat there; my mom was in bed, unable to talk, and she probably didn't even know what was going on at that point. The rest of my family was around the room and most of them were in a state of stupor because they didn't know how to respond. They didn't know what to say or do. They were in shock.

I sat there and I thought the only thing I knew how to do was to give my energy to the Divine, to ask the Divine to help me in this situation, and I did Ho'oponopono. I sat there in the chair by the bed and I said in my head, *I'm sorry, please forgive me, thank you. I love. I'm sorry, please forgive me, thank you, I love you.* It was the only thing I knew to do. What I was doing was creating a kind of prayer to the Divine, and I was saying, "Not my will, but thine be done. If there is any way to clean any program in me that is affecting her..." because remember everything on the outside is actually a projection of what's in you.

I looked inside myself, and I said, "Look, if there're any beliefs in me, any data in me, any programs in me that were causing this to appear on my outer reality, then take care of it in me." And I turned it over by saying, "I'm sorry, please forgive, thank you, I love you. I'm sorry, please forgive me, thank you, I love you." And as I did that, I felt better, which is really important because before that, I was angry, I was in grief, I was confused, and none of those were energies or modalities or mentalities that were helping anybody.

Eventually, I got to a place of peace and we all left when visiting time was over, and guess what? My mother got better. My mother went home. I'm convinced that because of this praying and clearing, my mother extended her life by five years. The extra time was priceless. I was able to talk to her, complete with her, and be at peace with her. She finally passed away on March 4, 2016, more than a half decade later than when we first thought. It was yet another miracle.

What I did was surrender. I surrendered to what I perceived to be the Divine. I'm telling you, this is where you create miracles because when you're not trying to do it on your own, you can get results.

I have heard of a lot of people getting results from just the techniques we talked about earlier, but now we're adding Ho'oponopono or anything you can do to create a connection with Divinity or God or the universe to help you achieve and attract what you want or something even better. And this stuff works.

The fourth stage of awakening, which I'll spend most of the last lesson on, is awakening itself. That is one of the most beautiful moments of anybody's life. We'll talk about that later in the book because we need to build to it, otherwise, it's just an intellectual exercise if we just talk about it now.

Eleven Ways to be Happy

We want to stay out of victimhood. One of the best ways to stay out of victimhood and to be in empowerment and surrender is to learn to be happy. When they flew me over to speak in Kuwait a few months ago, I put up this particular graph that showed "Eleven Ways to be Happy." One of them is to *practice smiling*. When you smile, your whole body and mind changes.

The energy flushes through your system and you suddenly feel better, even if you felt bad to begin with and you feel like you're forcing it; when you start smiling, grinning, even laughing, it feels great. So that's one thing you can do immediately.

Another one is to *sleep more*. That's a curious one because people don't know how powerful sleep is, but your body and mind demand it. You need to get proper rest. I'm a big believer in getting your six hours or seven hours, it might be eight hours for you, but you do need your sleep. I also like to take a nap during the day if I can find ten minutes for a power nap; man, that's like eight hours of sleep for me. A nap will make you feel better. You'll be more in tune with life and you'll have more energy if you sleep properly.

The next one is to *practice gratitude*. You've heard me talk about gratitude a lot. Gratitude is the single most powerful thing you can do in any moment that transforms you and that moment. Be grateful. Make it up to begin with if you have to, but find something to be grateful for—the water, the horseshoe, the glasses, the computer, this book, or whatever. Be grateful. Practice gratitude every day and it'll change your life.

The next thing that's on the list is to *help others* a couple of hours a week. This is really important because when you help other people, you are actually helping yourself. And that can mean anything from making a contribution, to being a volunteer, to doing some sort of cleanup duty. You do whatever feels right to you but do something to help out others.

The next one that's on the list of eleven scientific ways to be happy is to *exercise*. Exercise at least seven minutes a day. What they're talking about is some sort of cardio where you get your heart rate beating a little bit. You can jog in place. You can do jumping jacks. You can go for a walk. You can go for a sprint. You can go for a quick jog. You can bend horseshoes if you'd like. You can go to the gym. You can lift weights. You can do yoga. You can do Pilates. You can go swimming.

I know, there's all kinds of things but pick something and every day; do an exercise for at least seven minutes, as a minimum, and what it does is energize you. It makes you feel alive.

Right before sitting down to write, I got up and I bounced around the room a little bit and I shot my hands up in the air a few times because I was getting my energy up. Then I said a little prayer of cleansing, because I wanted to set the intention that I'd be totally here for you and that all the inspiration would come through me so I can really help you the best I can. So that's exercise.

Another one is to *go outside*. We live in this world where we're all incubated. We're all covered in these little boxes. I'm in a box right now. But I live on a lot of acres and I have a walking trail and I know how powerful it is to go outside. Go outside. Get some fresh air. If you go outside when it's a little chilly, great, because it's going to wake you right up.

So another one is to *move closer to work*. I don't know if you work at home or if you're driving to work but if you can cut your commute time down a little bit by moving closer to work, that'll actually help you and help you feel more rested. You won't be behind the wheel all the time.

Another one is to *spend time with family and friends*. Have some social time and I don't mean Facebook time, I mean actually getting out and being with people, having coffee with them, a drink with them, lunch, dinner, breakfast, going to a movie, having a conversation, having a party, going to a concert, or doing something with family and friends. Be social. It's good for your mind and body.

Another one is to *plan a trip* and you don't necessarily have to take it because there's a lot of excitement in just planning a trip. For example, I've always wanted to go to Switzerland, so right now, I'm thinking about where I want to go and what I want to see in Switzerland. There're some guitar makers over there. I want to see them. I know the watchmakers like Rolex are over there and a whole lot of wonderful people and great scenery and all that, so I'm starting to think about what it would take for me to go, and when I would go. And there's almost more excitement in planning the trip than in going on the trip. So plan a trip is another way to be happy.

Another one is to play the ukulele and that's obviously just for fun. *Pick up an instrument.* It could be a harmonica. I actually have a harmonica on my desk. I keep it with me all the time because I play harmonica. I have guitars around me. I have a guitar sitting right here. I do have a ukulele in the back. The idea is to play some sort of fun instrument.

I think it was Steve Martin, the comedian, who said, "When you play the banjo, everybody smiles." They all seem to love the banjo, which is similar to the fun of a ukulele. I don't mean go out and play professionally; just do it for fun. Do something that makes you feel good.

And the last of the eleven scientific ways to be happy is to *meditate*. And we've talked about that before but I think it's really important that you spend time, every day, quiet in your mind, observing your thoughts, but not being attached to your thoughts. Actually feel what it's like to be in a state of silence, in a state of being a witness.

Those are eleven different ways to help you be in the moment, for you to escape vulnerability, and to stay empowered and stay with surrender. Is this exciting or what?

176 · *THE MIRACLE*

Your Turn: The Secret Prayer

I wrote a book called *The Secret Prayer*, which I told you about, and in it I drafted a secret prayer, which I have also created an audio for. You can go to www.TheSecretPrayer.com if you want to listen to it, but I printed the words for it below. This is a way for you to surrender to the Divine.

What I'm going to ask you to do is think of something you are wanting to attract right now. Something that you want to have, do, or be. Just think of that right now. It could be the thing you've been thinking about all during the lessons or it could be something new and different right now.

If you want to go online and listen to this, it's only a few minutes long. But what it goes through is gratitude, a detached request, and an inspired action. So read or listen with that in mind and with the idea that you're saying this prayer to your connection to the Divine. It's called "The Secret Prayer" because it's a secret between you and the Divine. You don't have to tell me your prayer. You don't have to say your prayer out loud. Just follow along with this prayer and enjoy. It's only a few minutes.

The Secret Prayer

I'm going to lead you through The Secret Prayer. This is the prayer that always works. It is guaranteed to get results. All you have to do is relax, listen, and follow along. So let's begin.

First relax and breathe deep. Focus on being in the here and now. It's just you and me and this moment. Sigh and release all concern, all worry, all issues of mind. For the moment, you want to be here now. Feeling grateful for the now.

Wherever you are, notice that life is supporting you. Whether you are at home or in your office, at the beach or in the woods, your life is being supported by something greater than you. Call it God, Divinity, zero, the white board, or nature; this great something is pumping oxygen and blood through your body. Keeping your body, mind, spirit system alive and supporting the planet with things we often take for granted such as oxygen, gravity, and more. We are circling around in a solar system that is somehow keeping its balance and meanwhile our bodies are alive and keeping us here now.

Focus on this moment and all the wonderful things in it. The message is clear, something is taking care of you. There is much to be grateful for but you can focus on one thing to expand your gratitude. It can be the chair or bed you are on. It could be this recording. It could be your eyes for seeing and ears for hearing and your brain for understanding. It could be a loved one. Anything is allowed because you have the freedom to focus on anything you want.

As you choose to focus on gratitude and you feel the spirit of thankfulness expand within you, allow this warm feeling of love to fill your body and mind. You are living the miracle behind the theater of life with its ups and downs. All is well. All is good.

At the very source of life, all is wonderful and you are part of that wonder. You are loved. You are the miracle. Take a moment to really soak up this glorious feeling, because realizing the miracle of right now is the essential first step of the secret prayer.

And now, think about what you would like to have, do, or be. What would be cool to attract into your life? What would be fun? Let your mind deliver ideas and possibilities to you.

Don't censor anything. Allow it all to come into your awareness. You are simply playing with possibilities. As you think about all the wonderful things you can experience, allow one to come to your full attention. Which one of these possibilities feels like a heartfelt desire? Pick one to go through, this secret prayer, knowing that you can practice this prayer as often as you like and focus on different divine desires each time.

Now think of the mental equivalent of your desire. Imagine your desire being a real live experience. Describe it in your mind. See it in your mind. Do your best to playfully describe this desire so you can truly imagine it in your mind. Take a moment to find the mental equivalent of your desire right now.

And now Nevillize the desire by pretending that it has already come to pass. Your desire no longer exists in the future but is actually now part of your past. You have experienced it as real. What does it feel like to have, do, or be the thing you desired? Feel it right now. Take a moment to allow your desire to be a complete experience in your body and mind. Feel it real right now.

And now come back to this moment and realize that you've planted a seed with the great something. You have made a request.

You will be given signs and symbols, ideas and opportunities to help you bring your desire into reality. You promise to courageously act on the windows and doors that open for you. You have faith that all is working in your favor and every moment is bringing you to your desired result or something even better. To help you to accelerate the process, you will spend time in gratitude, feeling the miracle of this moment, and you will be aware and alert for the things for you to do next.

You promise to take inspired action. You promise to do your part in the co-creation of your life. And now you can end this secret prayer with a statement of gratitude such as "Thank you, thank you, thank you," or "Not my will, but thine be done," or "This or something better" or simply, "I love you." So be it and so it is, Amen.

Excellent. That is a very beautiful prayer called, "The Secret Prayer." Again, I wrote a book about it so if you want to read more, you can find the book on Amazon. This is yet another tool for shifting your consciousness as Einstein suggests.

The Mental Equivalent

I want to point out that I mentioned the "mental equivalent" in that prayer and I haven't described that in any of the previous lessons. Let me take a minute to do that right now because it's important. It's another tool to help you. This is another process.

The mental equivalent is a term that was created by Emmet Fox. He wrote a little booklet called *The Mental Equivalent* back in the 1930s. Emmet Fox is a very popular, very articulate new thought minister, and he's worth reading if you've never read him. But the mental equivalent means that when you want to attract something, you want to be able to have in your mind some sort of image, feeling, and thought about it. In other words, you have the mental equivalent to the thing.

It's one thing to say that you want to attract a particular car and you have a clipping of it or you have the catalog for it or you have a sales brochure for it, that's one thing. But what you want to have inside yourself is the mental version of it. So, as you think about the car that you want to attract (again, this can be used for anything: the relationship, the health, the money, the job, [fill in the blank], whatever you want to attract), you find the thought that corresponds to it, the feeling that corresponds to it, and the imagery that corresponds to it, and you create a thought form that's in your head that is the mental equivalent.

So a mental equivalent is like a brain-oriented symbol for what you want. That's the mental equivalent. It's a very powerful thing. Read Emmet Fox. Read *The Secret Prayer* and learn a little bit more about that.

Masterminds and Group Intention

I want to talk about masterminds and group intention because I said a little bit earlier that we (me, you, and all the other people around the world who are reading this) are all a group here.

As you're sitting there by yourself, you might feel like you're doing this all alone, much like I'm sitting here and I can't see all the people who are reading this at this point, so it feels like we are on our own. But when people are gathered together sharing an experience, they become a mastermind.

Napoleon Hill wrote about masterminds in his books *Think and Grow Rich* and *The Law of Success*. He basically said if three or more people all hold the same intention, that intention will come to be because the three people have a collective energy that is more powerful than the three people separately. So when three people get together, it's almost a fourth mind, not just the three minds, but almost a fourth mind in terms of esoteric energy.

Well, imagine what's going on here when we have all of these people—I mean it's staggering how many people are on to this. All of us can now jointly support each other in our intentions. And I want to tell you how powerful this is. For example, I mentioned a little bit earlier that there were the Texas wildfires and they were burning out of control and I had to surrender and I said I could do something and I did. I wrote an e-mail and I sent it to my mailing list.

Now, I have a database of people that are subscribed to my JoeVitale.com site. They sign up for my newsletter and then they start getting e-mails from me so they're on my e-mail list. I wrote to everybody on the list and I asked for a favor.

I said, "The fires are burning in Texas. I need your help to put them out and all I'm asking you to do is think positive, think rain, think health, safety..." and so forth. And I went on to say that there are twenty-four scientific studies that prove without any doubt that when people get together as a group, their intentions come true. And so I sent an e-mail out, telling people to stop the fires in Texas. Guess what? The fires in Texas stopped.

I did the same thing when Hurricane Rita was aiming towards Texas, including my house. It was coming this way. I sent an e-mail to my list and said, "Please focus on calm and peace and the dissolution, the watering down of Hurricane Rita." I asked my list to hold the intention. Guess what? Hurricane Rita dissolved. It went from a category five to a category one and it didn't even rain here. Hurricane Rita didn't come here because it turned into a rainstorm that didn't make it to my place. That's how powerful group intentions are.

And I told you when the floods took place, I wrote to my list and I did the same thing, "Please help my community recover from the sudden flood." People are recovering and they're actually joyous about it.

I told you about my mother. At that time, I wrote to my list and said, "Please help me hold the intention of the wellbeing for my mother." My mother got better so we could enjoy her presence for several more years.

We can help each other. This is a priceless moment for us to have a group intention and for all of us to hold the intention that each one of our individual intentions comes true.

And all you have to do is have that intention in your mind. You want to think good thoughts about everybody reading this book. You want to send positive energy. Just imagine the positive energy is going to everybody. You want to visualize it to the best of your ability; maybe visualize that people are participating in groups together or sending in comments saying how joyous they are and how they're dancing in the street because they're celebrating the achievement and the attraction of all their intentions.

We can do that for each other and we're doing it right now. Everybody is now holding the intention that all of our intentions come true. Is this powerful or what? This is exciting because I've seen that when groups of people get together, true magic happens.

Moving through the Stages

We're not victims anymore, so we're out of the first stage. We moved through the second stage of empowerment using every tool that we could come up with, including masterminds and group intention. We stepped into the surrender stage because we know we're not doing it by ourselves. We're doing it with the help of each other. We're doing it with the help of God, the Divine, the universe. We're doing it by invoking divinity.

While you're thinking about that, I want to introduce you to a very short song called *Invoking Divinity*. It's a three- or four-minute piece of music that Guitar Monk, Mathew Dixon, and I created and *Invoking Divinity* does exactly that. On the song, "I AM Prayer" from the *Invoking Divinity* album (which you can find at http://guitarmonks.com/invoking-divinity/), you'll hear me narrate a prayer or petition to the Divine to help all of us channel our energies to achieve our intention. I have printed the words below for you to read, whether you listen to the audio or not.

Invoking Divinity

I am the "I."

I am the "I," I come forth from the void into the light.

"I" am the breath that nurtures life,

"I" am that emptiness, that hollowness beyond all consciousness,

The "I," the Id, the All.

"I" draw my bow of rainbows across the waters,

The continuum of minds with matters.

"I" am the incoming and outgoing.

Of breath,

The invisible, untouchable breeze,

The indefinable atom of creation.

"I" am the "I."

"I" am the "I."

Common Questions

I would like to address questions others have shared with me about what you and I have been discussing so far—the three stages of awakening as regards to Einstein's Secret.

I'm learning the deeper activation of Ho'oponopono. Will it help all aspects of my life?

Absolutely yes. I promise you it will.

Step Five will be all about Ho'oponopono. What I learned about Ho'oponopono, the advanced Ho'oponopono, and how to activate Ho'oponopono will all be in that lesson. We've already gone over some of it and remember, as I write this, in my mind I'm doing the Ho'oponopono phrases. *I love you. I'm sorry. Please forgive me. Thank you. I love you. I'm sorry. Please forgive me. Thank you.* I'm doing it inside myself so I can be clear to allow inspiration to come in to help you.

This process is very powerful, and I assure you, all of the Ho'oponopono will dramatically change your life. I know this because I have heard stories from people with every issue you can imagine from health, money, relationship, job, employer, family, pet problems, and lost items. I don't care what it is, I have heard from people who have used Ho'oponopono with success for virtually everything you could ever possibly name, and that's the thing you want to remember. It works.

I have been practicing Ho'oponopono while participating in this process. The problem is, I have been down with the flu and a cough since the beginning of the process. I haven't manifested anything as of yet. I am open, and I do want to heal my diabetes, which is at a beginning stage. I also want a lot of money and better relationships. How can I get it all?

My response is that first of all, you will get it all. You might not get it all right at this moment, but by changing *you* in this moment, you will begin to attract some of it *into this moment*.

I find it interesting that you say you've came down with the flu right at the beginning of the process because sometimes our brains play tricks on us. We go into self-sabotage. We make ourselves ill to try to resist change and so you want to talk to your body and you want to talk to yourself and ensure it that what you're doing is for your highest good. You're not doing anything here that's detrimental. You're not doing anything here that's hurtful.

You are doing this process to help you expect miracles, live miracles, manifest miracles, and so forth. That's all good. As we go through all of the processes I've already taught you, and the entire Ho'oponopono process, and other ones we go through in the following chapters, you will learn more and more about how to manifest what you want, but to begin with, you want to heal yourself.

You want to love yourself. You want to appreciate yourself and you want to recognize that what you're doing is a really good thing for yourself. However, you have to pay attention when somebody gets the flu. Just look at the word flu, F-L-U. It suggests that they're trying to run from or flee something. Perhaps they're trying to flee a problem or a challenge in their life. They're trying to, in a sense, escape from what they're facing. That's the flu, an attempt to fly away.

Realize that that's a trick of the mind. But it's actually a form of self-sabotage, and you don't want to do that anymore. You want to love yourself. Appreciate yourself. Approve of yourself and wholeheartedly jump into this because it's good for you, and you know it, and that way you'll take care of your health.

With this process, you'll breathe easier, you'll feel better, and the energy will go through your system. You'll be able to feel the love of the universe come to you and through you the more you appreciate yourself, and from there, it'll be easier for you to heal your diabetes. It'll be easier for you to attract a lot of money or anything else that you want, but it starts right here in this moment.

I was reviewing the session on counterintention, and I feel a little bit lost regarding why the intention we set didn't happen yet. You said, "The explanation you give for an event is the belief that attracted the event." I don't quite follow that one. I've been trying to manifest something for the past two years and it has not happened yet. I do believe that it is possible I am blocking it to happen on some level, but I believe also that the Divine mind has a reason for it. Bottom line, I don't know why it has not manifested yet.

Well, I do have thoughts on the subject. It is admitted right there in the question, "I believe it is possible I am blocking it."

Right? "I do believe that it is possible that I am blocking it to happen."

That right there is what you want to look at. If you use the Socratic Questioning process that I taught earlier, you could begin with that. For example, in that line that you believe the manifesting is being blocked on some level, I would ask, "Do you believe you're blocking it?"

You would probably say, "Yes," because you said it in your questioning.

So, the next question is, "Why do you believe you're blocking your own good from coming to you?"

From there, your answer is going to be a little bit more filled because you're going to describe your reasons for believing it to be true. You would then question your own reasons and ask yourself if you believe those reasons. If you say, "Yes," the next question would be, "Why do I believe those reasons?"

What you're doing is dissecting your own belief.

I also noticed in the question the belief that it's possible that the Divine mind has a reason for you not to have what you want. My philosophy is the Divine mind wants you to have, do, or be *whatever you want.*

The Divine mind is not blocking you from your own good. The only person who would block you from your own good is you. That said, there is such a concept of divine timing, meaning sometimes you want something to take place, but the universe and all its wisdom can see more than your ego can see. Your ego and my ego can only see so much of the picture. The universe sees the whole infinite world of all possibilities and it knows when would be better timing.

One way I explain this idea is this: if I gave you a seed and said, "Turn it into a tree," you wouldn't be able to do it without planting it, without watering it, without making sure no weeds grow around it, and most of all—without waiting. You would have to wait for it to grow because it has its own divine timing. Sometimes that's the case, but you've got to be acutely sensitive so you don't deceive yourself and fool yourself because you don't want to sit there and say, "Oh I'm totally fine and I'm just waiting for the Divine to bring it to me." That's probably a form of self-deception.

> *"The Divine wants you to have whatever you want. It's a matter of you being okay with what you want."*

You want to know what you want, you want to be clear of everything that is in the way of getting what you want, and you want to take inspired actions to help pull into being the very thing you want. Never blame the universe by saying, "Well, the Divine doesn't want it for me."

The Divine wants you to have whatever you want. It's a matter of *you* being okay with what you want. So again, this is a great question. You should ask yourself these same questions to see how they relate to you. Ask yourself, "How does this become relevant to me?"

What do I do with my anger while I'm going through all of this?

Thank you for being honest about what you're going through. I'd say if you're feeling anger right now, you want to tap it away. Now, we've gone through a lot of different programs here, but the easiest one that I would give you right now is the *tapping technique* on anger. You would do the tapping as I described before (or as you find in *The Tapping Solution* by Nick Ortner or other EFT source), and you'd say, "Even though I am angry, I deeply love, accept, and forgive myself." And you would say it three times.

And then you would take the key word, a key belief, like anger and you would tap through the remaining points. And you may have to do that two or three times. Each time is called a round. But I would do two or three rounds and then notice how you feel. It should calm down—the energy should release.

The back-up technique to do would be to ask yourself, "Where's the anger coming from? Why do I feel anger?" And start to do a *Socratic Questioning* process and the *root cause erasing* process that we talked about in the last chapter. Those can help unearth the real reason for the anger.

And don't forget, with anger or fear or other issues, do *Ho'oponopono* because that's a process that works on an unconscious level. It's a petition to the Divine to help erase whatever is causing anger or fear or whatever. This is for you, no matter what your question is, to be saying to your connection to God (and you don't have to say it out loud but you say it inside yourself), while feeling whatever the issue or problem is, "I love you. I'm sorry. Please forgive me. Thank you." And you're basically saying, "I'm sorry for whatever my rage is. I have no idea what the belief is or where it came from. Please forgive me for being unconscious to the whereabouts of this belief. Thank you for erasing the belief from me. I love you for healing me."

That's the long form of what you're saying. We'll go into this in much more depth in the next chapter because that's all about activated and advanced Ho'oponopono, but you can do the four phrases now. "I love you. I'm sorry. Please forgive me. Thank you" on any of these questions, so keep that in mind.

I can't seem to create a mental picture or really feel what it would be like to have what I want. Right now I'm focusing on creating a loving relationship with my body and myself.

That's very good to create a loving relationship with yourself. Now, depending on what you want, there's a lot of different ways to manifest it. I often use the example of a car and if you really can't imagine having a new car or driving a new car, go to the car dealership and drive one.

Just do a test drive. Tell the car salesman you're thinking about driving this car and you want to do so. Then you'll be able to see it and feel it and experience it and you'll have that in your brain. If for some reason you can't do something like that, another way to do it is to watch a movie about somebody who is doing it. Watch somebody who is living the life you want or a character who you really admire and as you're watching them or the movie, you're seeing a visual right there, so there's the mental imaginary. And then you just imagine what they're feeling or what you're feeling as you're watching it, which will move you closer into the mental equivalent of what you want to attract.

Once you clear a subconscious negative belief, can it return? Does one constantly need to clear?

Those are two different questions, so let me break it down. "Once you clear a subconscious negative belief, can it return?" No. If you have cleared the belief, if you actually cleared the main root cause belief, no. It will not return because it is gone. This is so important to get and this is why you want to keep cleaning and clearing because as you're doing it, you are getting freer and freer.

You know, the person that I was when I was homeless and when I was in poverty is not the same person who is sitting here, now, living the lifestyle of the rich and famous and enjoying so much of the great wealth and richness and spiritual awakening of life. But how did it happen? I kept cleaning myself, and as I cleared the limiting beliefs in my brain and they left, they left for good. That's also true for you. When you clean it, it is gone for good.

Now, the other part of the question is, "Will we have to keep cleaning?" Yes, most likely because there is so much data in the world. There are so many negative beliefs in the world that we'll probably have to continue to clean, but the good news is we know how. We have all the tools here. And as we clean, we get happier, we get healthier, and we attract more of what we want; it just gets better and better.

If you truly have cleared the limiting belief for good, is the reason it appears to still be present because there is another limiting belief still present that you haven't uncovered?

Yes. Exactly. This is why I said in my book, *The Attractor Factor*, that when you get the lesson, you no longer need the experience. It'll go away.

The reason we keep having problems reoccur is that there is a belief behind them. When we get rid of the core belief, that root belief that I talked about last chapter, then that experience will leave and there will be no remembrance of it; it'll be gone. You'll barely even remember it. You'll remember it as a story that has no emotion on it because it doesn't happen anymore.

I'm good for a few days after each lesson, but then the old mindset starts settling in. How do I maintain this new way of thinking?

That is a great question. You want to participate with other people who are holding our intentions to make a difference and have all of our individual intentions come true. But it would also be really good to do something every day to remind you of this. Do the meditation every day.

Do the gratitude every day. Earlier in this chapter I went through eleven scientific ways to be happy now—pick a few of those or do one every day so you stay congruent. That'll keep your energy up and keep you in the flow.

Einstein's Secret Revealed

I'm doing my best to give you this experiential learning experience so that you actually feel what I'm talking about and expand your mind so that we actually live what Einstein was pointing to and we leave all of the lower levels of consciousness and move into a state of awakening, which is wonderful and miraculous.

Einstein says we cannot solve the problem with the same level of consciousness, or the same mind that created it. What I'm teaching you is how to leave the mind that created it. That's the secret.

You want to leave the mind that's been creating your problems so that you can get out of it to a higher level of consciousness. We're living *Einstein's Secret* by leaving that dimension or mindset, which is usually on the victimhood plane where people created their problems. That is the whole purpose of this particular lesson. That's what we're doing. The second stage is empowerment, and lucky people like you are now in it. The third stage is surrender, and we have learned several processes for doing that.

Up Next...Step Five

Step Five on our path to enlightenment is all about Ho'oponopono. I'm going to tell you stories. I'm going to tell you about Dr. Hew Len. I'm going to tell you about the basic Ho'oponopono, advanced Ho'oponopono, and then we're going to activate the Ho'oponopono. I'll talk about the traditional Ho'oponopono and I'll break it all down. Remember, miracles happen when people use the Ho'oponopono process.

The next chapter is going to be a fantastic turning point. And remember that you're not alone. You've got a whole group that is here, with you, and we're all holding the intention that our intentions come true. Mine, yours, and everybody else's. That's an overwhelming power. So *expect miracles*. *The Miracle* is coming your way. I love you. I appreciate you and I will see you in the next chapter.

Deep Within

As you prepare to flip the page for the next chapter, I would like to share a song with you called "Deep Within." It is a slower song off my last singer-songwriter album called *One More Day*. It's referring to the soul, the spirit deep within you. If you have the album, play it as you follow along with the words. If not, just absorb the words as you read them.

For now, enjoy "Deep Within." Thank you. Thank you. Thank you.

DEEP WITHIN

Words and Music ©2015 by Joe Vitale. All rights reserved.
www.AllHealingMusic.com

deep within
past my mind
it resides
...heaven

past my thoughts
past my soul
deep within
...heaven

way beyond my mind
way beyond my thoughts
sits a soul deep within
...always on watch

> look within
> feel it so
> that's the world
> you want to know

deep within
past it all
sits a soul
in charge of it all

deep within
past my eyes
there is something
oh so wise

deep within
past my mind
in my heart
all is fine

> look within
> feel it so
> that's the world
> you want to know

STEP FIVE

Expect Miracles

Something amazing happens when we surrender and just love.
—Marianne Williamson

Welcome to session number five in *The Miracle: Six Steps to Enlightenment*. I hope you've enjoyed applying what you have learned thus far. If so, I'm sure a lot has been going on for you.

In this session, we are going to go even deeper and talk about one of my favorite subjects. We're talking about inspiration. And we're going to focus primarily on Ho'oponopono. You know a little bit about Ho'oponopono from the previous chapters we've gone through, but now I want to take you into the land where nobody has gone before, except me and a few other people. We're going to go deep into that.

We've covered a lot of ground in this book, everything from my story to talking about at least three of the stages of awakening. We've talked about victimhood. We've talked about empowerment. We've talked about surrender and we will continue to talk about surrender in this chapter, but we're going to focus on how to use surrender as a very productive, healing, miraculous approach to living. And you're going to love it!

Also, I want to congratulate you for doing all of this. I want to applaud you because we've been covering so much material and you're hanging in there. We are working with these different stages of awakening and all these different techniques for finding what beliefs are, for cleansing beliefs, and for removing beliefs. We're doing a lot but you're tracking with me; you're working on yourself. So I applaud you.

Common Questions

I want to start by answering questions that most people have at this point. It's good to address what might already be on your mind, before we jump in to the next session. I hope it will be helpful for you.

While I say Ho'oponopono, do I concentrate on one of my desires or on my issues?

It's entirely up to you. You can focus on whatever you want. I'll tell you from my experience, most people focus on an issue. They focus on a problem, mainly because that's where most people's minds are. Their minds are focused on problems. It's very much a sign of victimhood mentality because of instead of coming from solutions or following Einstein's quote about leaving the consciousness that actually created the problem, most people stay on the same level of consciousness that created the problem. They stay as a victim thinking about the problem and they keep wrestling with the problem.

Most people use Ho'oponopono on their problems. There is nothing wrong with that. It's a way to dissolve the problems. It's important to realize that you can do whatever you want with Ho'oponopono. I've had people use it for every single thing you can name. I don't care if it's pet problems or financial problems, or health, relationships, jobs, anything you can name, people have used Ho'oponopono, the four phrases, on those problems to help dissolve them.

It's also important to realize that when people are working on their problems with Ho'oponopono, they're not working on the problems; they're working on their perceptions of the problems. That's a key difference for understanding how to surrender and awaken so you can *expect miracles*. We want to go beyond the mind that's creating problems. We want to actually clean up our own consciousness and clean up our perceptions—that's what Ho'oponopono does.

Now, at the same time, some people use Ho'oponopono on their desires. So if you are desiring a soul mate or a better job or your small business to do well or to have increased income, you can do these statements on those desires. I would say that the rule of thumb is pick one thing, problem, desire, or whatever it happens to be, and use the phrases on that one thing.

In this chapter, we're going to go into how to activate Ho'oponopono so it can work even better for you and go even deeper for you.

Can you give us specific examples of how Ho'oponopono has changed your life?

Absolutely I can, because I've been doing Ho'oponopono for over ten years. When I first learned it, I wrote about what I was doing in the book *Zero Limits*, and then ten years later in the follow up book called *At Zero*. There's more information in those two books about what I've done in my own life.

Now I use Ho'oponopono all the time. I use it for everything. Before I created this for you, I wanted to make sure that I was totally present with you; that my mind wasn't wandering, that I wasn't thinking about something from earlier today or something that I'm doing afterwards. I want to be here with you. I want to be clear inside so I can more or less channel the information that's specifically useful to you. So I set the intention of saying to myself, "Please help me be the clearest and the most present, so I can be of the most help and inspire these people who are reading (meaning you) to have, do, and be the miracles [you] want in your life."

At that point, I'm just saying, "I love you. I'm sorry. Please forgive me. Thank you," as a way of cleansing myself so I can be here with you. The "I love you. I'm sorry. Please forgive me. Thank you," which are the four key statements of Ho'oponopono, are helping me delete any beliefs, negativity, memories, programs, or any data that's in my mind that would prevent me from being here and being present with you so I can be of the most help to you. That's an example of how I'm using it right now.

Ho'oponopono for My Body

I remember the first seminar I attended with Dr. Hew Len, when I first learned Ho'oponopono, I was getting a urinary tract infection in my body. I was just learning about the four phrases and I thought, *Well, let me try the four phrases on what's going on in my body*. And as I was lying in bed that night, I was saying, "I love you. I'm sorry. Please forgive me. Thank you," as I was thinking about the body infection. In the morning it was gone. So that was one of the very first times that Ho'oponopono changed my life.

Ho'oponopono for Healing

If you remember the last chapter when we were talking about surrender and Einstein, I told you the story of my mother. Several years ago, she was dying and she was in intensive care, in the emergency room, and I sat beside her and I said the four phrases in me. It's important to realize that I didn't do the four phrases *to change her*. I did the four phrases *to change me*, knowing that as I changed, it would enable her to do what she needed to do, which could be to pass or could be to get better. As it worked out back then, she got better and that was five years ago. My mother has since passed, but we had five or six extra years with her, and that's pretty miraculous in itself.

Ho'oponopono for Peace at Home

Another story that I haven't talked too much about (so this will be a fresh one for you on how I've used it myself) is about my home. I live in the country, in Texas, and there are a few acres beside me that have been vacant for ten years. And I've liked it vacant because I have my peace here. I can go out and do a meditation out on my deck, up in the trees, and nobody is next door to distract me.

But then, one day, the people who had bought the property next door started to build a house on it. They came out there with their construction crew and started putting ribbons around trees that they were going to cut down and it greatly distressed me. I was admittedly not at peace over this. And I remember thinking to myself that there's got to be a way for me to find peace and be okay with them building or to find a way to stop them from building. I actually tried to buy the property and they didn't want to sell it. They had their hearts set on building a home there.

Since that wasn't working, the only thing I knew to do was Ho'oponopono. I was feeling my frustration and I was feeling my intention and I was waiting for inspiration to come. I kept thinking *I wonder what the divine solution is? What's the win-win?* I always look for a win-win-win in relationships and in business.

So I started doing Ho'oponopono. "I love you. I'm sorry. Please forgive me. Thank you." I'm saying it inside myself. I'm saying it to my idea of my connection to the creator. I'm not saying it to the neighbors. I'm not saying it to anybody else. I'm not even speaking it out loud, it's all internal. I did Ho'oponopono, and over time I felt a little better.

Then, inspiration hit. That's what we're talking about in this chapter—inspiration. Inspiration hit me and I had this *aha!* experience and a light bulb went off in my head. I suddenly had this wild idea and I jumped online to see if there was any property available for sale in my general area. I discovered there were four acres for sale down the street.

So I called the realtor who was selling those four acres and I said, "I have a wild idea. I think I can make two sales for you if you make one phone call and you're good."

She said, "What—what do you have in mind?"

I said, "The people next door to me are starting to build a house. They're on two acres. Call them up and tell them I will buy those two acres for the price of the four acres down the street."

So all these people had to do was stop their building next to me, sell the land to me, move down the street, and double their lot. Instead of having two acres, they would get four acres. This was an inspired, divine solution. They did it. They sold those two acres to me. Now, I paid more for the two acres than what somebody else might do because I paid the price of the four acres that were for sale down the street, so I paid double or triple for these two acres. But notice, these two acres beside me are worth a million dollars to me. They're worth a million dollars to my peace of mind.

I actually put a walking trail on those two acres. We will never build anything there. We will never cut trees down there. And I have a walking trail, so I can walk through the woods. When I go out to do my meditation, everything is peaceful. That is miraculous. That is a win-win-win and that came from inspiration, which came from me doing Ho'oponopono.

I have all kinds of stories about this, but other people have stories better than mine, most of which are in my book *Zero Limits* and in the follow-up book *At Zero*. Those books are at Amazon and at the library. You can read them for free.

If I identified a problem and now want to release it based on the many tools you shared already, where should I start?

That's a great question because we have covered a lot of material. You have a lot of things at your disposal that you can grab and use to handle anything that comes up in your life. What would I do if I had a problem occurring to me?

The first thing I would do is look for the belief that caused it. I'd ask myself, "What do I think the meaning is for this event?" And whatever the meaning is, it is most likely the belief that attracted it. So I'll start there and I'll find the belief that attracted the event.

Then I'll do the Socratic Dialogue and I'll say, "Do I believe this belief? Do I believe the belief?" And if I do, I'll say, "Why do I believe this belief?" So what I'll do is go through the process that we covered in step three, and I will investigate like a good loving, unattached detective trying to find with curiosity where the belief came from.

Meanwhile, I would be doing Ho'oponopono on the belief. I'd be saying, "I don't know where this belief came from but I'm sorry... please forgive me... thank you... I love you." Meaning, "I'm sorry for wherever the belief came from, because I don't know if it was my heritage, my ancestors, my mother, my father or who; please forgive me and forgive them. We didn't know what we were doing." We're primarily unconscious people anyway. "Thank you for removing the belief," and then finally, "I love you for taking care of me, and for my life."

You can say those phrases in any order. They don't have to be "I love you. I'm sorry. Please forgive me. Thank you." You can mix it up and go with whatever you feel. We'll talk about that a little bit more, later in this chapter.

And then finally, if the problem/belief is still bothering me, I would probably add the tapping technique. And that's where I would say something like, Starting at karate chop point, I'd be tapping and going through the cycle that we've talked about previously. I'd say, "Even though I still have this belief, I deeply love, accept, and forgive myself," two or three times, and then I would tap through the other points while repeating the belief.

That is the process I would probably go through.

I often feel that other people are bringing me down. I know that I am responsible for creating this, but I still have a hard time changing it. These interactions seem to lower my vibration. Any tips?

I do have a tip or two; one of the tips is consider changing your friends. I did a promotion recently and there was somebody who really wanted to invest in a coaching program. His friends were telling him, "Oh that's only for losers." He was getting depressed about it because he really wanted to get into coaching. His friends were pulling him down. And I thought to myself,

"You really need to *up* your friends. You really need to be with people who are far more supportive of you."

If you happen to be around people who are not very supportive, then be protective of your dreams. I am a big believer in protecting your dreams. I'd be selective about who you talk to about what you want to do because if people tend to "rain on your parade," so to speak, it's better to stay away from those people. That's the first tip: I would consider being protective of yourself and upping your friends; be around people who are more supportive.

The deeper approach to this—and I've referred to this other times with other questions over the previous chapters—is realizing that those people who seem to be bringing you down are voicing your own beliefs. A part of you unconsciously believes what they're saying, so there's an opportunity for you to clean up your beliefs. Those people are acting as a mirror. They are reflecting what you, on a deeper level, actually believe. So you want to clean up your own beliefs. When you do, those people are probably going to leave your life, never say anything, or become champions of your cause. They'll start to be cheerleaders rather than people who rain on your parade and try to put you and your dreams down.

Surrender and Ho'oponopono

Now, as a reminder, we're talking about level three, surrender. We talked about victimhood; we talked about empowerment, and now we're talking about surrender with the focus on Ho'oponopono.

I know you may know what Ho'oponopono is, but not everyone does. So forgive me if I repeat myself a little bit but I want to talk about Ho'oponopono and the famous story behind it because this story is the most amazing, most miraculous, and most inspiring thing that I have run into in my life so far.

About twelve years ago, I heard this story of a therapist who somehow healed an entire ward of mentally ill criminals without seeing any of them. When I first heard the story, I thought, *Oh that's preposterous. That's got to be an urban legend. That couldn't happen.* And I blew it off. I just thought, *No, that's not real.*

I heard the story again a year later. People would say, "Have you heard about that unusual therapist? He did some kind of unusual Hawaiian technique and he healed all of these mentally ill murderers and rapists, these criminals who were locked away in a mental institution—but he didn't actually do any traditional therapy, he did some sort of magical, esoteric spiritually-based therapy."

I said, "Well maybe I should check it out 'cause if it's true, then the world needs to know."

If it's true, *I* needed to know. So I went looking, and at that point, there was no information. I searched all over the Internet. I looked under every rock. I looked through books. I couldn't find anything on this. So I started making calls. I even hired a private detective, at one point, to try to find this therapist. Long story short, I found him. He was living in California at the time and his name is Dr. Ihaleakala Hew Len.

I always called him Dr. Len for short, even though it's more accurately Dr. Hew Len. But Dr. Ihaleakala Hew Len is his name and I called him up. He was very nice to me. He didn't know me at all. He didn't know my name. He didn't know what I wanted, but I asked him questions. I said, "I've heard this story..." and he said it was true.

I said, "But how could you work at a hospital for mentally ill criminals who are being shackled and sedated every day—a dangerous environment where the doctors keep quitting and the nurses quit because they don't want to be in such a hellish situation?" I said, "How did you go there and what did you do?"

And he said he was called to go there because they were desperate to have a licensed therapist on staff. They needed it by the State. Nobody else wanted to work there and Dr. Hew Len said, "I'll take the job but I'm going to do my own brand of therapy." And what he told me was he didn't do therapy. He said, "Therapy doesn't work." And he said therapy was already proven not to work with these criminals that were in the insane asylum. He said that they were being sedated and they were being shackled because they were dangerous. They would actually leap out to hurt people. He said that people would walk down the halls, the corridors, of the hospital with their backs against the wall, just kind of shuffling down so that nobody would reach out and attack them. And Dr. Hew Len went there.

I asked, "Well, what did you do?"

He said, "All I did was clean."

"What does that mean?"

He said, "All I did was clean on my perceptions of what I saw."

"What does that mean?" None of this made sense to me.

He said, "Have you ever heard the phrase that you create your own reality?"

And I said, "Well yeah, of course, I actually say it. I actually write about it. I'm one of the people who gets on a soapbox and writes books saying you create your own reality."

He said, "If you create your own reality and somebody shows up in your life that is a mentally ill criminal," as they showed up in his life, "didn't you create them too?"

My head exploded at that point. I suddenly realized that he was talking about a level of creation and a level of responsibility that almost nobody goes to. We all, at some point, when we go into an empowerment stage, we all start to feel, "Yeah, I'm responsible for me. I'm responsible for what I say, I'm responsible for what I do, but I'm not responsible for you or you or you or you or anybody else."

Dr. Hew Len said if you're creating your own reality, then you also created that person, that person, that person, and me. He really was stretching my mind.

I tried to understand, but it was only a phone call. It lasted almost an hour, but towards the end, I could tell he was getting tired. He invited me to go to his seminar. I paid for my friend who had told me about Ho'oponopono to attend the seminar with me (he didn't know anything about it either). And together we met Dr. Hew Len. It was the most mind-altering experience. He talked about thought forms being real, like the thoughts in your head actually are energy vortexes and they float out into the world and actually create reality.

He also talked about being 100% responsible for your life—meaning you're responsible for everything in your life. It doesn't matter whether it's the neighbors who start to build a house next door or it's your parents or your employer or employee—on some level you're creating it. You're responsible for that.

That's part of what he was talking about. But he really honed in on only four phrases. And he said the four phrases are "I love you. I'm sorry. Please forgive me. Thank you." As simple as can be. "I love you. I'm sorry. Please forgive me. Thank you." And I couldn't believe it. My mind was skeptical. It's like you're changing mentally ill criminals with this? That's it?

As I spent more time with him he answered all of my questions. We ultimately spent a lot of time together; we led three seminars together. We co-wrote the book *Zero*

Limits together. He came to my home. He stayed here in the city with me. We had dinners. We had coffees. We did a lot of exploring.

I asked a lot of questions and ultimately I learned that when he was working at that hospital, he would look at the people's charts—he would get a chart of a client or patient—and he would read it. As he was reading it, it would stir up feelings in him. He'd be upset. He'd be frustrated, angry, embarrassed, or enraged, depending on what he read.

He used Ho'oponopono to cleanse those feelings *in him*. He didn't clean the patient. He didn't clean what he was seeing in the records. He didn't clean their photo. He didn't clean the individual. He cleaned himself and his perception of what he was seeing.

This is really important in understanding Ho'oponopono. It's not about correcting the other people. It's about correcting your perceptions of everything you see outside. And here's the thing that happens, when you take care of your perceptions, they get better.

This is what happened to Dr. Hew Len; he's looking at his files, he's feeling upset, he's cleaning up his feelings, and he's cleaning up his perceptions, and the patients got better. Ultimately, within a very short time, they started to be released. They didn't have to be shackled. They didn't have to be sedated. They started to be released having been determined to be healthy enough to go back into society. After four years, that ward was closed. It's a miraculous head-spinning story about the power of these statements.

Here is how Dr. Hew Len defines Ho'oponopono:

Ho'oponopono is a profound gift, which allows one to develop a working relationship with divinity within and learn to ask that in each moment our errors in thought, word, deed, or action be cleansed. The process is essentially about freedom. Complete freedom from the past.

That's it. That is Dr. Hew Len himself, telling you what Ho'oponopono is, and it's about correcting perceptions.

I want to go a little deeper here (I wrote about this in the book *At Zero*, so please read it at some point), and talk about how to use the four phrases of Ho'oponopono for maximum impact.

The way to make this work for you is to find something that is bothering you or triggering feelings within you that you would like to resolve, and apply the four phrases to it in a more intense way.

Your Turn: Ho'oponopono for Maximum Impact

You can do this right now; pick something that's bothering you. It could be something that happened today or something that you've been carrying around for the last seven days and you haven't gotten rid of yet. Choose something that's making you a little upset or is aggravating you a little bit. Identify something that you'd like to resolve or clean up or delete. Find something you'd like to change, knowing that if you change this one thing that your life will feel better. It could be a situation like I had with the neighbors bothering me when they were going to build next to me.

If nothing comes to mind, perhaps you could pick a desire. Choose a goal that you're going after or something you want to attract. The idea is to pick one thing that has a little energy on it. And by that I mean you can feel it in your body that you're not quite at peace with it. If it's a problem bothering you, it's aggravating you a little bit, and if it's something you desire, you have that energy of joy because that's what you want.

Once you have identified something that stirs up feelings in you, here's how it works. Feel the feelings inside of you. That's where the feelings are—inside of you. They're not outside anywhere. They might, as an illusion, seem like they're being triggered by something on the outside, but it's really inside of you. So you look inside of yourself and feel that emotion.

As you feel it, talk to the Divine in your mind. This is just pretending. You pretend that God is listening to you. You pretend that the Divine is listening to you. Or you pretend that you're talking to your higher self or nature and you say, "I'm sorry for whatever beliefs I inherited or absorbed from my ancestors or myself. Please forgive me for the data or the beliefs or the memories that are making up this feeling of frustration (or whatever the feeling is). Thank you for deleting this data, these negativities, these programs, this negative perception out of my body and mind. I love you for healing me, for giving me life, for taking care of me, and for making me whole."

Honing In

What you're doing when you use the four phrases of Ho'oponopono for maximum impact is honing in on one thing. This is much like when Dr. Hew Len was in his office looking at one chart. He didn't look at the file cabinet. He pulled one chart out and he looked at it, and as he was feeling what was being triggered by what he was seeing, he knew that the trigger and the feelings were in him. They weren't in the chart. They were in him. And that had nothing to do with the other person. The other person didn't even exist in some ways because all he was looking at was the paperwork, not the other person.

So as he was looking at the paperwork, he's feeling what he's feeling and that is what he is cleaning and clearing on.

This is powerful. This is why I do it every day because things show up out of the nature of life.

Who Taught the Teacher?

Let's move on here and make this work even more. Dr. Hew Len is the man who taught me Ho'oponopono, but who taught him? He learned it from a woman named Morrnah Simeona who is considered a national treasure in Hawaii. There's a statue of her. An honorary wreath has been given to her. She is said to be enlightened.

She actually went to the fourth stage—the stage of awakening—and she is said to have upgraded Ho'oponopono into the spiritual activating healing mechanism that we have today.

You see, there've been two Ho'oponoponos. In the early days, for hundreds of years, maybe more, there was a Ho'oponopono that was done as a group effort. Whenever there was a problem in the community, the people would gather together like a tribe and sit in a circle and an elder, like a chief, like a father figure, like a priest, would guide the whole circle. People would take turns saying what their grievance was and asking for forgiveness, and they would stay in the circle until peace had been achieved among the whole tribe or circle.

That's the old form of Ho'oponopono and it's still used today in Hawaii and other places. But Morrnah had an enlightening experience and realized that you didn't need all the other people. She realized that if you had a problem, it had nothing to do with the other people; it had to do with you.

In fact, Dr. Hew Len at one point told me, "Have you ever noticed that when you have a problem, you are there?" Sounds pretty funny.

Have you ever noticed that when you have a problem, you are there? You're the common denominator. You're the person that's participating in all your problems, but until now you didn't realize that you were the one creating and attracting them on an unconscious level.

You're not doing this purposely. So you can't blame yourself. You can't feel guilty. You can't punish yourself because you didn't do any of this to yourself with any intent. It all came because of unconscious programming.

So Morrnah came to earth and she told all of us, and especially Dr. Hew Len, "You don't need the other people. You don't need a group. You can do it inside yourself."

And she came up with her own phrases; four of the phrases, "I love you. I'm sorry. Please forgive me. Thank you," are the four we use all the time. They're the four that I wrote about in my two books, and they are the four that Dr. Hew Len even uses today. He's now retired and doesn't travel or speak anymore, but he's alive and well and spends most of his time cleaning and clearing—the thing he thinks he's on earth to do.

Morrnah came up with her own prayer and it is a system for separating memory from inspiration. Let me address that real quick because in any one moment, you're either coming from memory or you're coming from inspiration. Almost all of us are coming from memory.

Now what does that mean? It means that in your head there is a database of beliefs and your unconscious mind, which is far bigger than your conscious mind. There's an entire programming structure, an entire software program that has been wired over generations that you inherited with epigenetics from your grandparents and great grandparents. All of this has come down from generations and has been formed in your brain so that together when you act in any moment, most of what you're doing is based on your memories. It's based on your beliefs.

It's based on the database in your mind. It's not based on the purity of the moment because you have all of these beliefs filtering out what you see. What you want to do with Ho'oponopono is remove the filters. When you remove the filters or remove beliefs, then inspiration can hit.

I'm in love with inspiration. I've often said, "Intentions are for wimps." I want inspiration. What I mean by that is when you clean up the beliefs and you're able to be in this moment, at that point, inspiration can come in and tell you to act. In my case, it told me to become a musician five years ago and start making music, and now I have fifteen albums out. That wasn't an intention; that was an inspiration that I then made an intention. You see the difference?

Chapters ago, I told you a lot about intentions, and intentions are powerful. Intentions are better than being a victim and having no intentions. But what's better than intentions? Inspiration. When you get an inspiration, you can let that be your new intention.

For example, I recently held up a horseshoe and I told an audience that I bent it. I told them that it was a symbol that *nothing is impossible* and somebody asked, "Why are you bending horseshoes, except to prove that you can do it?" And now what I want to say is, "I'm now bending bolts."

I have a bolt that is an example of what I bent recently—I bent the bolt with mind power, will power, muscle power, and endurance—this is real. It was straight and I bent it. Why? Because I was inspired to. I am being inspired by strong men feats of strength, and for me, at this point in my life, it is a thrill to do it. I am loving it. I am loving learning how to take a nail and with my mind and my will and my muscle (you've got to use your hands), bend it. Life is a co-creation. You don't do everything with just your mind.

You use your mind to will your muscle and the rest of the world to come and make something happen. So I'm bending metal to prove nothing is impossible and it's one of the most exhilarating things I can do with my life. That may do nothing for you. You may have no interest whatsoever in bending a horseshoe or a bolt or a nail or a steel bar and you don't need to.

The point is, as you get clear of the data and the filters and the beliefs and the memories and you're in the moment, then the thing that makes your heart sing inspires you. That's powerful. It probably won't be bending horseshoes, but then again, maybe it will be for somebody reading this book. More importantly, it is probably going to be something that is unique to you; something that is exciting! That's when your passion comes alive! That's when your exuberance for living comes alive! That's when your energy just shoots way up and you realize you can have, do, or be anything, because you're following inspiration.

And inspiration has no limits. Memories have limits. When you start having data come up and it's filtering your moment, it's based on the past. It's not based on what's possible. It's based on what you know you could do that's been done before.

Inspiration can melt all limits and inspire you to do things that are unimaginable to you now and to the rest of the world, like bending a screw. So this is where we're going and I get excited about this because I realize at this point we can become super humans. We can become Gods walking the earth, and I don't mean that in an ego-way. I mean that in a fully actualized way. But you actually become this integrated whole person that is using spirit and mind power and body power and will power and divine power as one, all coming together and then going out there and achieving miracles, which is why this book is called *The Miracle*.

Your Turn: Morrnah's Prayer

So here's what I want to do next. I would like you to take about five minutes to read *Morrnah's Prayer*. Or, you can go online to http://guitarmonks.com/morrnahsprayer/ and listen as I read the prayer to you (with the music of Guitar Monk Mathew Dixon in the background). This is a prayer that Morrnah wrote. It's designed to help you melt any of your beliefs or any of the things that are bothering you. If you listen to this, you'll come to a place where you'll hear me tell you to insert whatever the feeling is that's bothering you right now. So if you have something that's still bothering you, or something that you would like to create in your life, just use this prayer to go through this little exercise. Pick something and insert a feeling or a belief that you would like to remove or release or clean or clear or delete.

Morrnah's Prayer

I am the "I." I am the I. I come forth from the void into the light, I am that emptiness, that hollowness beyond all consciousness, the I, the Id, the All. I draw my bow of rainbows across the waters, the continuum of minds with matters. I am the invisible, untouchable breeze, the indefinable atom of creation. I am the I.

Spirit, Superconscious, please locate the origin of my feelings, thoughts of [fill in the blank with your beliefs, feelings, or thoughts that you want to have erased]. Take each and every level, layer, area, and aspect of my being to this origin. Analyze it and resolve it perfectly with God's truth. Come through all generations of time and eternity healing every incident and its appendages based on the origin. Please do it according to God's will until I am at the present, filled with light and truth, God's peace and love, forgiveness of myself for my incorrect perceptions. Forgiveness of every person, place, circumstance, and event, which contributed to this, these feelings, thoughts, and beliefs.

Peace be with you. All my peace. The peace that is I. The peace that is I am. The peace for always. Now and forever and ever more my peace I give to you. My peace I leave with you. Not the world's peace but only my peace. The peace of I.

Oh, that's so beautiful. That's *Morrnah's Prayer* and I hope you felt as deeply cleansed as I did while reading or listening to it.

Activating Ho'oponopono

Next, I want to talk about activating Ho'oponopono. It's one thing to say the phrases, "I love you. I'm sorry. Please forgive me. Thank you," saying them in any order that you like, saying them inside yourself, and saying them to your connection to what you think is your Divine or divinity.

Dr. Hew Len always said you didn't really need to feel what you were saying; you just needed to say them. My suspicion was he said that because he knew that if you kept saying them, you would start to feel them and that led to the discovery, on my part, that you get faster results with Ho'oponopono when you activate it.

How do you activate it?

By feeling the words themselves. When somebody says, "Please forgive me," and they just say the words, they're just three words. "Please forgive me. Please forgive me." No meaning. No emotion. No connotation. No energy on them. "Please forgive me."

But what if you actually felt what the words were meaning? In other words, you really go inside and you think to yourself, "Oh please, please forgive me. Please forgive me." And genuinely feel it. And if you did that with every one of the phrases, you would activate Ho'oponopono and throw a switch that would just burn through any negativity, any limiting beliefs, any of the memories that were holding you back from expecting miracles.

To activate Ho'oponopono, feel the phrases.

When you say, "Please forgive me," it's not just please forgive me. You don't just say, "Please forgive me." You feel "Please, please forgive me." Or when you say, "Thank you," instead of just saying, "Thank you," and being polite, you say, "Thank you!" You want to feel the gratitude, real gratitude behind it, like "THANK YOU! Thank you so much! Thank you! Thank you for my life!"

And that's the same with "I love you." If you were telling your date or your spouse "I love you," and turned and walked away, there would be no connection. There would be no emotional fire. What you want to do is feel the love when you say, "I love you."

If you were really talking to God or you were really talking to the Divine, would you just say, "I love you," and keep going? You would probably look at them or feel them in your soul and go, "I love you. I love you."

It's the same with any of the phrases, "I'm sorry." Instead of just saying, "I'm sorry, oops I bumped you. Sorry." That's polite but it has no energy to it. It has no feeling or emotion to it. So when you say, "I'm sorry," you want to really feel "I'm sorry. I didn't mean that. I am so sorry."

So to activate Ho'oponopono is to feel the phrases as you say them within yourself. This will put a lightning rod in the words and it will shake the words with thunder and it'll make the phrases actually work faster and better and stronger than just saying, "I love you. I'm sorry. Please forgive me. Thank you." Obviously, just saying the phrases are going to help because they help so many people for over a decade that I've been able to chronicle in my two books. But when you activate the Ho'oponopono, my experience is you're going to get results that much faster.

Your Turn: Activate Ho'oponopono

What I want you to do next is activate your Ho'oponopono. I encourage you to visit http://guitarmonks.com/enlightenment/ and download *The Enlightenment Audio*. This is music created by Guitar Monk Mathew Dixon and me and it's about twelve-to-fifteen minutes long.

I recommend this because it is the perfect audio accompaniment to activating Ho'oponopono. While you say the phrases over and over again in your mind, activating the Ho'oponopono in your mind, *The Enlightenment Audio* also has the four phrases as a subliminal within the message.

This means that your conscious mind is not going to hear *I love you. I'm sorry. Please forgive me. Thank you*, but your unconscious mind is going to hear it. And then, at the very end of *The Enlightenment Audio*, I will speak a Sanskrit clearing mantra. I'll first say it in Sanskrit and then I'll say it in English and you'll know it's ending at that point.

Here is what I say in Sanskrit, followed by the English translation:

AUM BHOOR BHUWAH SWAHA,
TAT SAVITUR VARENYAM
BHARGO DEVASAYA DHEEMAHI
DHIYO YO NAHA PRACHODAYAT

Translated into English:

Oh Supreme Creator, thou art the giver of life, the remover of pain and sorrow, and the bestower of happiness. Oh Creator of the universe, may we receive thy supreme sin-destroying light. May thou guide our intellect in the right direction.

So after you have the audio ready, what I want you to do is close your eyes, and focus on something you want to have, do, or be, or focus on something you want to remove (a memory, belief, or database). Just focus on being in the moment, because this moment is *the miracle*. You want to *expect miracles* and be in this moment, and *The Enlightenment Audio* is designed to bring you there. So close your eyes and relax to the music. Don't think about a whole lot of stuff. If you do, just let it come and go. Take this time to activate Ho'oponopono: *I love you. I'm sorry. Please forgive me. Thank you.* Feel the phrases. Let's do that now.

Following Inspiration in Music

On *The Enlightenment Audio*, I was playing what's called a synthophone, which is an alto saxophone turned into a MIDI-instrument (it has digital electronics to connect to synthesizers and computers), and why was I playing it? Because I was inspired to. I didn't have an intention to play a synthophone. I could play a regular saxophone. I could play a guitar. I could play a harmonica, and I did on that tract, but as Mathew and I were exploring music, somehow or other divine inspiration led me to a synthophone, which I had never heard of before. But I followed my passion and I followed the clues. I followed that moment and it led to something that was mind altering because some of the music we created sounds like waves and things in the background, but they were made with this instrument that I had never heard of before.

This is an example of how intention versus inspiration works. When you're in the moment, inspiration can come to you, and then you can make the inspiration an intention rather than trying to make it an intention from your ego, and then try to make the intention control the universe. We want inspirations to come first and then turn those into intentions. How do we get to do that? By practicing Ho'oponopono.

So that's what we've been doing in this particular step, which has covered a lot of material. We've really gone in depth with surrender and Ho'oponopono. In the next chapter, we'll be talking about awakening and I have some real treats for you there. You're going to love the stories and the processes when we get to them.

But for now, I'd like to address questions that people often pose to me at this point. I want to be the most service to you by anticipating some of the issues or questions you may be having right now.

Common Questions

Is forgiveness necessary? Would we ask forgiveness for the happy feelings? This is what I'm confused about.

No, you don't have to ask forgiveness for happy feelings because those aren't anything that you want to remove. Those aren't anything that you are finding wrong. Happy feelings, passionate feelings, uplifting feelings, exuberant feelings, and wonderful feelings—bring them on! Hug on! Own them! Share them! Those are fantastic.

The feelings that we want to have forgiveness around are the feelings that bring us down. They are the resentful feelings, anger feelings, rage feelings, embarrassment feelings, shame feelings, and regret feelings. You know what feelings I'm talking about. Everybody does because the feelings that lower our energy, lower our vibration, and in fact make us not feel happy, those are the feelings we want to forgive. We want to forgive ourselves and whoever we perceive to have wronged us so that we can be in this moment and be happy in this moment. So it's not about getting rid of any unhappy feelings, it's about welcoming the happy feelings, and being forgiving around the energies of the feelings that aren't happy.

How can it be that if you change your perception—for example of a person—the person himself changes?

That's how it works and I'll give you an example. Let's say you are in a relationship with your husband, and you feel angry about something he did three days ago. You know he didn't put the toothbrush back. He didn't put the toilet seat up or down or whatever is the preferred way, and you're holding that as resentment. You don't have to say a word. He will feel it, right?

He's going to feel that you're upset about something, even though you haven't named it yet. And because he feels that you're upset about something, he's going to react to you differently. He may actually want to fight with you. He may be on guard with you. He may walk out and just want to get away from you for a while. Any number of things.

So what if, and here's the opposite, you're at peace? You're loving. You're happy and you look at him with gratitude and unconditional acceptance. He will feel that. He will respond to the way you feel. But again, you didn't say anything. All you did was change the inner you. So this is how it works.

When you change the inside of you, you're changing your beliefs, you're changing your perceptions, you're changing your mindset, and you're changing your memory. When you change all of that, you will act differently. You will send out a different vibrational signal and everybody around you will respond to you differently because they're responding to the new you. That's how it works.

If you think about it, you can probably come up with examples where you walked into a room and somebody across the room—you didn't even know who they were—but you felt a standoffish kind of feeling from them like, "I don't want to talk to that person." Or you walked into a party and there was somebody over there in a corner and they're smiling big and looking happy and talking and everything and you wander right over. Why? They are sending out signals through body language and a few other things, but without actually having to say anything. You are responding to it. When you change yourself, other people respond to you on that unseen energy level.

If I keep on repeating the four phrases without thinking of any problem or desire, will I be getting rid of my problems and issues?

Absolutely, yes, and that's a great question. Because I've been doing Ho'oponopono for over a decade now—I am doing it right now even as I write to you—in the background of my mind, the tapes are going in my head,

"I love you. I'm sorry. Please forgive me. Thank you. I love you. I'm sorry. Please forgive me. Thank you." It's the new background talk. It's the chatter in my mind as I'm writing to you and when I go to sleep at night, it's still going on as I'm sleeping I'm sure the tape is going all night long. And so I don't need to have a problem and I don't want to have a problem to trigger me doing it. I do it so I don't have a problem to work on.

"When I do Ho'oponopono, it's like a street sweeper at night. It goes out in front of my moments and cleans them so that when I get there, there's no issue."

My metaphor, or the imagery that I think of is in some big cities they have street sweepers and snow blowers that come out at three o'clock in the morning and clean the streets. So while you're sleeping, the streets are all cleaned up of trash, sand, dirt, snow, and ice. In the morning, when you get in your car and drive, the roads are clean and you don't think anything of it. When I do Ho'oponopono, it cleans my pathways, the roads of my life. When I do Ho'oponopono, it's like a street sweeper at night. *It goes out in front of my moments and cleans them so that when I get there, there's no issue.* There's no problem. I can be in the moment. So I'm doing Ho'oponopono all the time, whether there's anything to do it on or not, I'm doing it as habit in the moment.

I would like to know how long one should focus on a particular intention before moving onto a new one: just once or until it materializes? I've heard people defending both of these positions on different occasions. What's your take on this?

My take on this is that you do it as long as it's fun. For example, right now I'm writing another book and I have a strict deadline to have it done. So my intention is to get that book done, to get it done on time, and to make it the best of my ability. I'm not just thinking about that intention once; I think about it every day because it's high on my mind and it is something that I want to make sure it is achieved and attracted and is as perfect as I can make it by my deadline. So I'm not just doing it once.

But sometimes, if you feel like you've stayed in intention and you have cleaned on it and you let it go, you don't need to think about it anymore. It's really a personal choice. For me, I find that focusing on three intentions is more than enough at any one point. So I'll focus on two or three intentions on any one day, at any one point, and I'll just cycle through them and put a little energy on each. When I say energy, I mean happy feelings.

Right now, I'm thinking that I'll finish my book by my deadline. It's called *The Awakened Millionaire* and I'm focusing on how great it will feel. So my intention is to have that happy feeling—that feeling of accomplishment, the feeling that I attracted this intention and completed it on time and I'm feeling that now. And

I'll feel it tomorrow and probably every day right up to the day it is due. Then I'll probably have another intention after that; I'm not sure what yet, because they just show up as inspiration.

So I suggest that you focus on intentions as long as it's fun. You don't want any of this to feel like work. It should feel like play. It should feel like, "Man I can't wait to Nevillize my goal. I can't wait to do affirmations. I can't wait to do a belief process." It should have that kind of a feeling to it.

What if I have more than one problem or desire at the same time; how can I do Ho'oponopono for both? Is it possible?

Absolutely, yes. You can do it for everything. You can list everything and you can go, "Divine, I've got these four problems here. I've got a money problem, a health problem, a relationship problem, and a job problem. Please forgive. I love you. I'm sorry." Do the phrases on the package deal. The title of this is *The Miracle* and we want to really come from the frame of mind that anything is possible. Why would we think that we can only do one problem or one desire? We live in a world where we can do anything!

If you have three or four or five or six things going on, put them all in a package, pretend they're all wrapped up, and then do a Ho'oponopono session on it. Listen to *The Enlightenment Audio*, practice activated Ho'oponopono, and do it on all of it. It doesn't have to be one thing. If one has a lot more energy on it than other ones, I would go there first. Meaning that if you're really upset about one of four things, I'd pick the thing that you're really upset about. But you can do it on all of them at the same time. There's nothing wrong with that at all.

Should we set deadlines for our intentions and goals (from inspiration)?

Yes, if it's from inspiration, definitely.

I mentioned my goal to write *The Awakened Millionaire* with a specific deadline, but it depends on my intention. It depends on my inspiration. It depends on how I feel.

I think having a deadline for a goal is fine as long as you're willing to move it. Some people get so obsessed with a date that they can almost hurt themselves or feel unhappy or unhealthy trying to meet it. You want to be happy. You want to be in the moment. You want to appreciate everything that's going on in your life. So if it feels good to set a date, great. But if you get to the date and you need to move it, be okay with moving it. Trust yourself.

As I wrap up this chapter, I want to share the lyrics to a song called "Got a Problem?" It's my Ho'oponopono song that I wrote for my very first singer songwriter CD, *Strut!*. It's a song a lot of people like. We call it "The

Ho'oponopono Song" because it's about realizing that we're all one and any problem you have and I have, it's all the same. We're all in the same boat here. You can grab your own at AllHealingMusic.com.

I want to thank you for being here because I love you. I appreciate you. I'm grateful for you. We are doing this together. We are co-creating. Remember to do something for *you* every day until you finish reading our next lesson on awakening. That's the fourth stage. The awakening stage.

Godspeed to you. *Expect miracles.*

Here is the song "Got a Problem?"

GOT A PROBLEM?
(THE HO'OPONOPONO SONG)

Words and Music ©2012 by Joe Vitale. All rights reserved.
www.AllHealingMusic.com

Say you got a problem.
I got one, too.
Say you got a problem.
Now we got two.

I'll take your problem,
make it go away.
I'll take your problem
and erase it today.

> I'm sorry. [I'm sorry]
> Please forgive me. [Please forgive me]
> Thank you. [I love you]
> I love you. [I'm sorry]
>
> I'm sorry,
> please forgive me,
> thank you,
> [I love you] I love you.

Mirror, mirror on the wall,
who's the fairest of them all?
Mirror, mirror on the street,
who's that we always seem to meet?

I'm sorry. [I'm sorry]
Please forgive me,
thank you,
[I love you] I love you.
I'm sorry,
please forgive me,
thank you,
I love you.

Ever notice when you have a problem you are there?
Ever notice when you're in love you are there?
Ever notice when it's raining out you are there?
Ever notice when the sun is shining you are there?

The secret, you see,
is you are free.
The secret, to me,
is you are me.

[I'm sorry] I'm sorry. [Please forgive me] Please forgive me. [Thank you] Thank you. [I love you] I love you. [I'm sorry] I'm sorry. [Please forgive me] Please forgive me. [Thank you] Oh, thank you. [I love you] I love you. [I'm sorry] I'm sorry. [Please forgive me] Please forgive me. [Thank you] Thank you. [I love you] I love you. [I'm sorry] Oh, I'm sorry. [Please forgive me] Please ... [Thank you, I love you] forgive me. Oh, thank you. [I'm sorry, please forgive me] I love you. [Thank you, I love you]. Oh ... [I'm sorry] love you. [Please forgive me, thank you, I love you] Oh, I ... [I'm sorry, please forgive me] ... love you. [Thank you, I love you] I ... [I'm sorry, please forgive me] ... love you. [Thank you, I love you] I ... [I'm sorry, please forgive me] ... love you. [Thank you, I love you] [I'm sorry, please forgive me, thank you, I love you, yeah].

STEP SIX

The Awakening

*If every day is an awakening, you will
never grow old. You will just keep growing.*

—Gail Sheehy

Welcome to the final step in *The Miracle*. I am excited for you, proud of you, and I congratulate you, and me, because we did this together. This has been quite a ride. Isn't it amazing that it seems like it was only a few minutes ago that we started step number one and now we're on the final step, number six?

We've covered so much ground that it's really amazing. We'll reiterate and recover a little bit of what's relevant from the previous chapter to get into this one, but in my mind and my heart this is the most important lesson of all of them. Everything was leading up to this moment because what we were doing in all the previous lessons were talking about all the stages before awakening.

This one is about the actual awakening. It is the most powerful, the most empowering, the most divine, and the most top of the Everest experience that we can have as spiritual human beings. This is where we're all going. I say that life is a process of awakening and what we're doing through this book is awakening. That's how powerful this process is and that's why I'm so excited.

Common Questions

Before we begin the sixth step, I have to tell you I'm overwhelmed with all the wonderful compliments, positive reviews, feedback, gifts, and everything that has come my way as I have shared this information. What you are now learning in this book has moved so many people. Thank you for the gifts, testimonials, endorsements, praise, and now, thank you for the questions. These questions are all relevant because they represent what everybody is thinking. Use my responses to deepen your understanding.

How do I do continuous cleaning through Ho'oponopono?

It's very easy. All you really do is remind yourself to do it.

Now, when you first start doing it, what you can do is write notes on yellow stickies to remember to do the cleaning, remember the four phrases, and even write the four phrases down, "I love you, I'm sorry, please forgive me, thank you."

Tear off the sticky, put it on your computer, put it on your phone, put it on your refrigerator, and put it on your mirror. Stick it someplace where you're going to see it.

Put it on the dashboard of your car. Put it on your desk at work. Put it on your mouse. Put it on your water bottle. You can put it anywhere. You can put it on the back of your phone. What I'm suggesting is that you just make a reminder and after a very short period of time, you'll find out that you don't need the reminder anymore because it'll become second nature to you.

When you start to meditate in any form and you start to do the Ho'oponopono cleansing phrases, it may feel unusual at first. It feels uncomfortable only because it's a new habit, but as you keep doing it, you create this new wiring in your brain and the synapses start to create new roads. Soon it becomes the new habit for you and is no longer strange. Now it's normal. That's how it is for me.

Now, of course, I've been studying Ho'oponopono for well over ten years but when I first started out, I got a yellow sticky. I put them everywhere reminding me to say, "I love you, I'm sorry, please forgive me, thank you, I love you, I'm sorry, please forgive me, thank you." I would say it inside myself; say it to my connection to God. Now I don't need a reminder. It's going on automatically right now as I write to you. So it's become second nature for me. Make it easy, just have a reminder.

What other ways besides watching my thoughts and feelings can I uncover my limiting beliefs and root causes?

There are lots of other ways for watching your thoughts and feelings. A lot of them we covered in the second, third, and even fourth steps. If you go back and review those, you'll see that they're there. What you need to do is to become sensitive to what you're thinking and what you're feeling and ask yourself, "What are the beliefs behind what I'm thinking and what I'm feeling?"

For example, a while back I had given you the idea that whenever you get upset, it means a belief in you was triggered and you went unconscious. That's why you got upset. It didn't have anything to do with the other person, with the situation, or whatever you blamed it on. It didn't have anything to do with that. That was the trigger that flipped the switch in your brain that activated a belief that you probably weren't even aware of.

So what you need to do is use all of life's experiences, moment-by-moment experiences, to discover your beliefs. When you discover your beliefs, then you want to use a lot of the processes we talked about earlier to question your beliefs, tap away your beliefs, find the root cause of your beliefs, and actually use Ho'oponopono on the beliefs.

You now have a lot of different tools to use but you want to become aware of your beliefs. All it really requires is alertness, sensitive, mental screening of your thought process and the feelings that come up, and constantly asking yourself what the belief could be that makes you think that way. *What could be the belief that makes you feel that way? What could be the belief that makes a particular event happen in your life?* That's how you increase the awakening.

It seems as I have applied the law of attraction over the last few years, the things I would like to have—but not given much thought—come easier than the things I most want and have given the most thought. Is this common and if so, how do I make a positive change for the things I want most?

This is very common. The reason it's common is because when you want something really bad and you think about it really bad, you're putting on an energy that's actually pushing it away. Now why is it pushing it away? It is because you're putting too much energy on it and it's energy of desperation.

Look at it this way. If you say that, "I'd really like to have so and so experience" and it happens easily, it's because you didn't have any mental interference. You didn't have what we talked about in an earlier chapter—a counterintention. But if you said, "I really want to have something," and you focus all your energy on it, and all your thoughts on it, you really send every kind of vibration you can think of to it. Why are you working so hard on it? Because underneath your work, you don't think it was going to happen. You've put too much of a demand on it and underneath the demand is the sense of desperation.

Now all of this is in layers. Most of us don't know this. This is why this book is so important. The average person has no idea about the law of attraction, and the average person who does learn about the law of attraction doesn't go deep enough to understand what you now know about counterintentions or negative limiting beliefs that are hidden from your conscious mind.

So it's always easier to attract something that you don't have a lot of energy on. If you almost flippantly said something like, "It'd be really cool if I had a brand new car by next Friday," chances are you would be moving in the direction of having a brand new car by next Friday, because you don't have a lot of energy on it.

Now, if you did something like, "I really want this brand new car. I would love to have it next Friday, so I'm going to script every day. I'm going to affirm every day and I'm going to Ho'oponopono every day. I'm going to go to bed at night and Nevillize that I have this car every day and I'm really putting on the after burners and I'm really going for this thing." You might be doing it with a sense of desperation underneath your momentum because why would you work so hard to try to attract it, unless underneath it you want it more than what you really are comfortable with?

In other words, you can almost always have something if you don't want it too bad. That's something to think about. *You can almost always attract whatever you want if you don't really need to have it* because if you need something, if you are addicted to something or if you're attached to something or if you're demanding about something, all of those are clues that underneath your conscious mind are some unconscious doubts and disbeliefs and scarcity thoughts about the very thing you want to have. All of this is good news because it's an opportunity for you to clear what's in the way of you having what you want. That's really important.

If your partner is clinically depressed and negative, and you are trying to stay positive, yet it seems the cycle of financial issues continues and they try hard to overcome that while dealing with post traumatic stress disorder, what advice can you give?

That's a great question and there's a lot here. If you're talking about somebody who's clinically depressed and negative, you're probably talking about somebody who needs to have some help. I don't mean that in any negative way.

We all have to remember that we have resources on this planet that are designed to help us. If I broke my arm or was in a car accident or something, I wouldn't sit around Nevillizing my well-being. I'd get to a hospital.

I'd get professional help. I'd say mend my arm, take care of whatever is broken from the car accident, take care of me, and mend me.

Then I would add Nevillizing or Ho'oponopono, tapping, and anything else I could think of, but I would start with the resources. We don't want to dismiss resources because we have limiting beliefs about, "Oh, I want to do it myself" or "I want to do it with the law of attraction" or "I want to do it the natural way." If somebody is hurting and they are in pain and they are, as you say here, clinically depressed, they need help. So I would arrange for them to get help.

There are lots of resources out there. Some of them are free. I would do some research. I'd Google it, I'd find out where are the resources for clinical depression. I'd read the books. I'd contact the help. I'd go to the social services. I'd do whatever was possible. Then for you, the person asking the question, the person who's not clinically depressed, you still need to do all the cleaning on what you perceive.

Think back to the story I told last chapter when I told you about Dr. Hew Len and how he went to the hospital for the criminally insane and in that hospital he saw all of these people who needed help. He was there to help them if he could but what he did was work on himself. When he worked on himself, those patients got better.

So you may be with this person who is clinically depressed and that person may need to see a specialist for the clinical depression.

Meanwhile, you want to clean on what you're seeing because as you clean your perceptions, you will help that person get better. That's an important lesson here. This is advanced teaching for most people. This is stuff most people never talk about; never think about; but here we are, going there because this is the session on awakening.

We really have to understand that we're leaving victimhood. We're leaving all those lower stages. We're going into a more empowered place to be. So my first thought is, don't dismiss help. If somebody needs professional help, make sure they get it. The second thought is be sure to work on yourself with all the different things we've been talking about.

How do premonitions work into all of this? I have flashes in my mind and when I get to it, I usually think of it as a premonition but now I'm wondering if I manifested it from that flash. Any thoughts?

I love these kinds of questions. This is actually a brilliant question because what you're getting a sneak peak of is the idea that the premonition and the creation are actually the same thing.

Now, again, few people out there in the world know this because they think in terms of either intention or they think in terms of premonition or they're not thinking of either one of them. They're just going about their lives and trying to survive. You have opened a little door here. You've opened a window and you have a peak into how the universe works.

When you have a premonition, more often than not, it's an insight that's coming from your unconscious mind about what's going to take place or could take place in the future. Yet, the other side of this is that premonition is actually an unconscious intention. You are actually creating the very thing you are seeing in the future. You're doing both of them. This is where life gets really interesting because in all the previous lessons and in the world out there, they think in terms of duality.

They think in terms of "me" versus the rest of the people, especially those in victimhood. They think in terms of, well, you can have a premonition or you can have an intention but you can't have both. The way the world works when you're awakened, is when you realize that we live in a non-duality universe that what we saw as separation, is not separate at all, it's an illusion.

Actually we're all one; we're all part of this illusion of life and even the premonition and the intention are two sides of the same coin or two sides of the same bubble and they're actually one. You're getting a sneak peak into where we're going. So with that, let's move even further into this because this is really exciting.

Moving Forward

In this segment, we're talking about the awakening. The awakening is the most profound experience you have. I love the quote by Carl Jung, the Swiss psychologist. He said, "Who looks outside, dreams; who looks inside, awakes." This is where I keep pointing in every one of the steps, with the last two and this one being the most important.

We no longer want to look out there into the world and say, "It's them," or "I'm separate from them," or "It's their fault," or in any way, shape, or form point fingers at them because that's still dreaming. *We're looking outside, so we're still dreaming.* What we want to do is look inside. We want to look inside of us and treat ourselves like the movie projector of our life.

---

*Who looks outside, dreams;
who looks inside, awakes.*
—Carl Jung

What we're seeing all around us is actually being projected from us. Your brain is actually a moving picture show and it's creating a script and it's projecting it into the world. What you see is your movie, but you don't usually know it, and you haven't known it up until now because it felt like your life, but it's your life as a projected movie. Now, where is the projection coming from? Your thoughts, your feelings, everything in your mind primarily, in the unconscious mind.

What we're doing in this final lesson is *awakening from the dream*. Now after you finish reading this book, you're going to go back into life. You're going to go back into society and you're going to go back home with your spouse. You're going to go back to work with your employer and employees. You're going to drive through traffic and everything. You have to remind yourself that, now, life is different because there will be a tendency to fall back into the old habits. The way for you to remember that you're now coming out of all of that is to remember the four stages of awakening.

The first stage is *victimhood*. If you find yourself complaining about other people, blaming other people, feeling like it's you against other people, you're coming from victimhood, and all you need to know is "I'm coming from victimhood. I don't want to come from victimhood. Let me go to the next stage."

The next stage is *empowerment*. In empowerment, you start to realize that you can set goals, and you can set intentions. You can write affirmations. You can Nevillize. You can visualize. You can meditate. You can write scripts. You have all kinds of tools like belief work that you can work on, and all the meditations that you can do. You can do Ho'oponopono. There are all kinds of things you can do so you're not a victim. Whenever you start to feel like a victim, just have a little switch in your head that goes, "Oh, wait a minute, that was in Joe

Vitale's book, *The Miracle*, and I went through all six lessons and I know I don't have to be a victim. I'm empowered!"

Empowerment is the second lesson. In that second lesson you have all kinds of tools. Go watch the movie The Secret again. Go read one of my books or follow Bob Proctor or Jack Canfield or Lisa Nichols or any of the wonderful people out there and go to their seminars. Listen to their audios. Enroll in my Miracles Coaching® Program. Do whatever it takes for you to stay empowered. That's the second stage.

We know by now that there's a third stage of awakening and the third stage is when you realize that *you don't do it alone* and you can't do it alone. I told you a couple lessons ago how I went through Texas, and we had forest fires here, and if I could have put them out by my intention alone, I would have done it. We had two floods here just a few months ago, and if I could have stopped the floods or if I could have saved my friends from losing their homes, I would have done it, but I couldn't.

At a certain level you realize that "I am empowered, I'm not a victim, but I can't do it all. I need to join forces with something more powerful than me." That's when you join forces with what I call the Divine. You can call it the universe, or God, or nature, or Gaia, or your higher power. You can call it the great something, but you know there's something bigger than you. You know there's something wiser than you. You know that there's something that's more objective than you. You know that there's something that sees all the different opportunities and options and choices for you that you don't see. That's the great something that you want to join forces with. One of the ways I am teaching you to do that is with Ho'oponopono.

You feel whatever is going on in your life, whether it's an upset, anger, an emotion, or a thought. Something has triggered you being out of the moment and out of happiness and you tune in within yourself and you talk to your connection silently. You talk to your connection and you say, "I'm sorry, please forgive me, thank you, I love you." We talked about what that actually means.

"I'm sorry for the beliefs that are in me that I'm not aware of. Please forgive me for what my ancestors might have downloaded into my own DNA or my epigenetics or my unconscious mind. Thank you for taking care of this and correcting my perceptions. I love you for my life. I love you for repairing me and cleaning me and clearing me so I can be whole and I can be in this moment."

That covers those three stages.

Then, of course, there's the fourth stage. So what is the fourth stage of awakening?

The fourth stage of awakening is when you merge with Divinity. The fourth stage is *when you become God*. Now please hear me out here because it's so easy for the mind to rush in and add interpretation or meaning to what I'm trying to explain here. What I'm really saying is in the fourth stage of awakening, your consciousness becomes one (non-duality, remember) with the consciousness of Divinity.

Divinity, God, lives and breathes through you in the fourth stage. Now, I need you to understand that you can't make the fourth stage happen. In all the previous stages of awakening, you can do something and awaken from it. When you are feeling like a victim, you can read a book, or you can watch a movie, or you can have the right person say the right thing, and you'll realize, "Oh yeah, I'm empowered, I don't need to be a victim," and suddenly you're in empowerment. In empowerment, there're all kinds of tools and books and audios and courses and seminars and magazines and apps even, to help you stay empowered. There are all kinds of tools to help you get there and stay there.

Then in the third stage, you have Ho'oponopono. You have surrender. There are books—I've written two of them, *Zero Limits* and *At Zero*—and there are apps. I even have a Ho'oponopono app on the iTunes store.

There are all kinds of tools to help you get and stay in the surrender stage, in the co-creation with the divine stage, but in the awakening stage, you can't make it happen because it comes by grace. *Awakening comes by grace*. You can prepare yourself for an awakening and you can have glimpses of awakening, but the awakening comes to you from God. The awakening comes to you from the Divine.

You can't make awakening happen because that would be your ego trying to get rid of the ego to allow the Divine to come through. You can't do that. The way the world is set up is that you prepare for the awakening and you prepare in a lot of different ways. I'm going to walk you through a couple processes in this chapter to help you do that. These are very powerful.

I'm going to walk you right up to the door of awakening and we're going to open that door so you can peek inside and feel and even identify with awakening. But whether you actually awaken or not, isn't up to me and it isn't up to you. It's up to the Divine.

The more you walk up to that door, open it, and taste and breathe the experience of awakening, the closer you'll come to the moment of enlightenment, the moment of satori, the moment of awakening. We want to prepare for that. Along the way you need to dissolve all the illusions: whenever the beliefs come up, whenever the upsets come up in life, you want to use all the tools we've talked about in all the previous sessions.

Remember the statement, "The meaning you give an event, is the belief that attracted it." That's one of the most profound statements that I've given in the past. I want you to realize that it's something to be aware of because in order to awaken, you can't drag around emotional or psychological baggage or past memories that no longer serve you.

I've said it over and over again, if you want to expect miracles, you need to be in the moment. The moment is where *The Miracle* is, but if we're drawn out of the moment because we're upset, then we're not going to be able to see the divinity of right now. We won't be able to awaken because we've got this dark cloud over us. Whenever something is bothering you or something has triggered you, you've got to remember that the meaning you give an event, is the belief that attracted it.

This helps you hone in on the belief so you can use any number of the tools we've been talking about to get rid of the belief—to actually let it go.

A Few Reminders

I have some other reminders here for you. The first one is, whenever you get upset, a hidden belief was activated and you went unconscious. The second is, the entire world is a mirror of what's in you. We've talked about that a little bit, but it's really important.

I've created products like *The Secret Mirror*™ and *The Secret Reflection* that are designed to help you realize that everything you see around you is a projection of what's in you. It's actually a mirror. There's nothing to be upset about. There's nobody standing there who needs to punish you or make you feel guilty or in any way feel wrong. This is a matter of awakening.

What we're doing is realizing, "Oh, I've had beliefs that created that experience and what I want to do is remove the beliefs so I have a cleaner experience of the now, of this moment."

Another reminder is that "Virtually nothing is impossible, the limit is mine." I've learned that, of course, from everything I've done in my life. From being an unpublished author to having fifty-some books out, to being an unrecorded musician and now having fifteen music CDs out, to being a person who was afraid of public speaking and now I've traveled all over the world to speak in front of thousands. I have now been in thirteen movies and I have been on *Larry King Live*, twice. I have spoken in Peru to 20,000 people. I have spoken in Russia and all over the world.

I've also done the *Strongman Training* that I've told you about, and I do things like take a screw or a bolt and bend it. For me, this is inspired action that reveals to me the power of intention and the power of inspiration but also reminds me nothing is impossible. We may not know how to do something right now, but with our mind we can figure out how, we can figure out a way, and we can figure out some process to get us there.

Remember also that, "The miracle is right now." I've said that throughout these lessons and it's the constant reminder that when you really understand that this is it, this moment is it, and then you will understand what the miracle is.

The miracle isn't in the past. You probably have some memories, and that's wonderful. The miracle isn't in the future. You probably have some things that you would love to have happen and you're desiring it, but in reality, *the miracle is in this moment*. The past isn't here anymore. The future isn't here yet. *All that's real is this moment*. The more you're in this moment, the more you're in the miracle, and the more you can expect miracles.

Let's go even deeper with this. You've heard me talk a lot about intention. I still love intentions. Before I got onto this lesson, like all the previous lessons, I stated the intention that I wanted to give a peak performance. I wanted to be inspiring and inspired, and I wanted to deliver information that makes a difference in your life and leads you to an awakening.

I stated that as an intention, but I also asked for divine inspiration. I said a little prayer: "Guardian angels, please give the most benevolent outcome with this last lesson, so I am at my best and I deliver the best. That I come across as inspired and inspiring and I lead everybody to an awakening in whatever way that needs to happen. Channel the words through me, inspire me, use me as an instrument for divine good and help me to write what needs to be said to help everyone today," meaning you.

I'm stating an intention and I'm also going with inspiration. My favorite way of doing these things today is to have an inspired intention. Instead of just stating an intention, I want inspiration to come and lead the way. The whole reason I'm interested in the *Strongman Training* and bending nails and horseshoes and all of that, is because I was inspired to pursue it and that may make no sense to you or anybody else.

That doesn't matter because I'm the one being inspired. So as I'm inspired and I realize, "Wow, I really want to know more about this and I really want to know how to use my mind to direct my body and I really want to know, are there any real limits in the world?" I suspect there are not. So I've been divinely inspired to do this. Then, under the inspiration, I set intentions.

I want to learn how to bend bigger and thicker nails and bolts and actually steel bars and I actually want to learn how to bend horseshoes. I can already bend some but I want to learn how to bend horseshoes into a heart shape. I want to learn what's called scrolling, where you bend a long, thick, steel bar that is five feet long into a work of art, which you can give as a gift to somebody.

So I've been inspired to pursue the *Strongman Training* but under it, my intentions are things like, "How can I learn how to bend nails and bolts? How can I learn how to bend horseshoes into heart shapes? How can I learn to bend a steel rod into a work of art that I can give as a gift to somebody or use as a fundraiser?" So you can see that I'm combining both of them.

Another technique that I invite you to do is to pause throughout your day and ask yourself, in the moment, what would be the most inspiring thing you can do right now. Just ask yourself, "What is inspiration trying to tell me, what does inspiration want me to do?" That's where you want to open yourself up for inspiration. You can even have inspiration meditations where you get quiet like when I get in my hot tub and I have my gratitude hour. I can let it be my inspiration time too, and I can make myself available to hear what is the inspiration for me.

You'll also want to be sensitive. I saw a quote from Ralph Waldo Emerson that said, *"we want to be silent so we can hear the whispers of the Gods,"* and that's what you want to do—be so silent that you can hear the inspiration because the inspiration is always there. There's always an inspiration trying to come in, but we may be busy with our mouths and talking so much that we don't hear it or we may be so distracted by television, Internet, a movie, and other people, life, stars, whatever, that we don't actually pay attention.

So you want to listen for inspiration because the inspiration can lead you to awakening. Inspiration is closer to God. Intention is closer to ego; inspiration is closer to God, and what I want is an inspired intention. I want God to tell me what the inspiration is and have me say, "Yes, I will take that on." I will then have sub-intentions that help me fulfill the inspiration.

Be In the World, but Not of It

So what I'm really talking about here, in order to be awakened, is to be in the world but not of it. You want to be in the world but not of it.

I was once going to write a book or record an audio program called "mystic in the marketplace." I often thought of myself as a mystic in the marketplace. What does that mean? It means that I'm actually in the world of serving, buying, exchanging, creating, sharing, and all of that activity, but detached just enough to know I'm playing a role. I'm playing a part.

It's almost as though I look at life like it's a theatrical experience. It's at a giant stage on planet earth and everybody's got a role to play. Some of them know they're playing a role, most of them don't. Most of them are acting out their roles completely oblivious, completely unconscious that it's a role. But when you awaken to the idea that it is a theatrical game and you're actually playing a role, then you don't have to take anything personally. You can go with the flow so much easier. You can be happier almost all the time and you are free in your mind to be able to see choices and opportunities in each moment. So there's great freedom and there's a great awakening that comes from being in the world but not of it.

Practicing the Presence of God

I wrote about this in my book, *The Secret Prayer*, and I'll give you the condensed version. In 1600s France, there was a monk named Brother Lawrence. Brother Lawrence devoted his entire life to what he called, "Practicing the presence of God." It was his prayer. It was his daily devotion. It was his moment-by-moment homage to the Divine.

What Brother Lawrence did was pretend that everything he said and everything he did was for God. He imagined that he was in the presence of God at all times, at all times, and what he was doing was practicing the presence of God in all activities. He actually worked in a monastery kitchen, and he treated the chopping of carrots or celery and the making of soup as if he was making it under God's witness and for God. This transformed his moment-by-moment reality.

Instead of being in the kitchen and tediously chopping up food (and maybe complaining about making his soup to serve people he liked or didn't like), all of that was rejected for this holy mental meditation of realizing everything was under the presence of God. He was practicing the presence of God. That was in the 1600s.

He wrote a handful of letters. He never wrote a book that I'm aware of. He did write a few axioms, or spiritual sayings, and in the 1800s, they were published in a little book called *The Practice of the Presence of God: the Best Rule of a Holy Life* by Brother Lawrence. You can find various versions or copies of it. There are modern versions of it. I have probably twelve different versions of it stacked up in my library. All the versions are the same, though some of the modern ones try to update the language. The whole point is if you live your life from this moment on, as if you are practicing in the presence of God, what would you do different? How would you think different? How would you feel different? How would you act different?

If you genuinely take on this feeling that you're practicing in the presence of God, it will transform your life into the miraculous. Life can no longer be the same if you realize you wash your car or you wash your hair under the presence of God. You do it with a sense of faith, love, completeness, and awareness that nobody else, including you, probably ever experienced. *The Practice of the Presence of God* by Brother Lawrence is exactly right.

I want to share an excerpt from the book. The language is a little awkward, but feel the energy of this because I'm sending the energy and I'm sure Brother Lawrence is too, even though he's long gone.

> *I have quitted all forms of devotion and set prayers but those to which my state obliges me and I make it my business only to persevere in his holy presence. Wherein I keep myself by a simple attention and a general fond regard to God, which I may call an actual presence of God.*
>
> *Or to speak better, an habitual silent and secret conversation of the soul with God, which often causes me joys and raptures inwardly and sometimes also outwardly. So great that I am forced to use means to moderate them and prevent their appearance to others.*

This man devoted his life to acting as if he was in God's presence in every sense of the word—thinking, feeling, acting, cooking, speaking, conversing, and all. Brother Lawrence gave that as a gift to all and that has influenced so many people.

It influenced a lot of the New Thought writers, Emmet Fox, Ernest Holmes, and a whole long line of people, including me, and now it's being passed to you. This is important because we're preparing for an awakening, and in order for you to prepare yourself for an awakening, there needs to be a more holy perspective coming out of you.

The Gift

Instead of having the perspective of vulnerability when you felt like a victim, or even the power and control feeling that comes from being empowered, or even the little bit of the surrender feeling that comes in the surrender stage, what you really want to have is this embodied presence of God who has given you *all of this*. Everything has been a gift to you. Your life is a gift. The air you're breathing is a gift. Gravity that's keeping you in your chair is a gift; the cells in your body, the heart that is pumping, the lungs that are breathing, and the kidney that is working is a gift.

Everything in you is a gift, and when you really feel the gift that has come to you without payment, without toll, just by birth, just by living, and just by breathing, you can be moved into an awakening. You can be moved into realizing that you can never repay this. It is a gift beyond all understanding.

We've talked about gratitude before but you need to understand that this is a level of gratitude that goes beyond being grateful for a pencil or a pen or being grateful for a pair of glasses. This is being grateful for the divine light that was given to you from the Divine. This is powerful. This is beyond comprehension and beyond my words to describe, but once you start practicing the presence of God, you move in the direction of the miraculous. It's no longer mundane—it's now miraculous. It's no longer just a moment—now it's the miracle. That's how powerful this is.

I'm going to give you a moment to take that in. Then I'm going to walk you through a short awakening meditation.

Your Turn: Witness/Awakening Meditation

This meditation is just going to take a minute. It ties in a lot of the things we've been doing together. I've even done a little bit of this with you before.

So right now, just take a breath and let it out. Ease into your chair and relax. You can keep your eyes open and focus on one spot. You can close your eyes if you like. Notice you have thoughts. We talked in the very first lesson that you have thoughts and you're always going to have thoughts.

You have about 80,000 thoughts a day; most of them, at least in the past, have all been the same. Now you're learning how to *What if Up?* your thoughts, and you're learning how to replace thoughts with Ho'oponopono—"I love you, I'm sorry, please forgive me, thank you"—but you still have thoughts. It's the nature of your brain. It's the nature of your mind. It's going to generate thoughts and it's going to bubble into your awareness. That's the human experience to notice you have thoughts.

You are not your thoughts, you have thoughts, but you are not your thoughts. Somehow you're separate from your thoughts. Somehow you're observing your thoughts. So just notice you're having thoughts. Like, *Hmm, they're coming and going, they're flying by, and floating by like clouds on a blue sky.*

So let's move to your feelings. You have feelings. You have emotions. Maybe you're happy, maybe you're in bliss, and maybe you're grateful. I don't know what your emotions are now, but notice you have emotions. You're not your emotions.

You can be a witness to your emotions like you've been a witness to your thoughts. You can say, "Oh, I have the feeling of gratitude, I have the feeling of bliss," but there's the "I" and there's the bliss. The *I* is observing the bliss. They're not the same. They're separate. You are somehow a witness separate from the emotion.

Now, notice you have a body, you have a physical body and maybe it's a little achy, maybe it feels great, maybe you're totally relaxed, maybe you need to stretch, or move your head, move your neck, move your back, lean forward, or lean back. You have a body.

Again, notice you have a body. You are not your body. You are observing your body. You can talk about your body. You can look at your hands and say, "I have a hand, I have an arm, I have a face, and eyes," but you're separate. There's the I, and then there's the body. "I have a body." You are separate from your body. You can observe your body. You can be a witness to your body.

So this is the enlightening question: *If you are not your thoughts and you are not your feelings and you are not your body, then who or what are you?*

I am going to tell you that you are the background witness—the witness that's observing the thoughts, the witness that's observing the feelings, the witness that's observing the body. That is the awakening stage. That witness is enlightenment. That witness is the same in you as it is in me, as it is in all the people from all over the world who are reading right now.

It's the same witness that is in all the other people on the planet. They may or may not know it. They may not know it, but that witness is the background source of life. The more you can attune yourself to that witness, the closer you get to awakening.

You can treat what I just did as an awakening meditation and you can do it on your own whenever you think of it. You can do it every day. You can sit there and say, "Okay, I have thoughts, let me get behind my thoughts" and you just observe, "Oh, there're the thoughts, there's that background to the thoughts, what is that? That's God, that's the Divine, that's the great something." And the more you can attune and identify with that background witness behind the thoughts, behind the feelings, and behind the body, the closer you get to awakening. Again, you can't make awakening happen.

I'm walking you up to the door. Knock on the door, open it up, peak inside, and there inside is this witness. That's the awakening state that we want, and the way to get there is to practice the meditation, practice the awakening, practice the presence of God, and it'll come by grace.

The Fourth Dimension Meditation

I have another gift for you. This is a meditation that is about eight minutes long in audio format. It's an advanced manifestation meditation using everything we've talked about to take us to what I'm calling *The Fourth Dimension*. You can think of the background witness to your life as another dimension. We'll call it the fourth dimension. While I know there are still things you want to create in your life, I want you to pick something right now, something you'd like to have, do, or be.

You might want to make a recording of your own reading of this meditation to the fourth dimension where you can create what you want and mold it into reality to show up in the third dimension, which is the dimension of reality that you and I are sharing right now. Or you can visit http://thefourthdimensionmusic.com/ to download the audio that Guitar Monk Mathew Dixon and I created for this meditation. Either way, I've given you a lot of material and I want you to process this; this meditation will help pull it together.

The Fourth Dimension Meditation

Relax.

Breathe in slowly and deeply.

This is your time. Time to relax. Time to let go.

You can notice your thoughts, but you aren't your thoughts.

You can notice your body, but you are not your body.

You can notice your emotions, but you are not your emotions.

You are the witness. You are the observer. You are the essence.

Mentally travel behind it all. Mentally become one with the essence of all. You are the fabric of the universe. You are the energy of all things. You are floating in the fourth dimension.

Imagine something you would like to have, do, or be. Pick one thing. Here in the fourth dimension become that thing. Enter the energy of the experience.

Spend a moment imagining you are what you would love to have, do, or be.

Now in your mind, pretend you have become the experience you want to attract. You are the energy of it. In the fourth dimension there are no limits. There are no rules. There are no boundaries.

Allow yourself to merge with what you would like to have, do, or be. Live from within it. Be the energy of it. Imagine that now.

And now focus on your health and well-being. Experience radiant health. Your body renews itself. Your body heals itself.

And now experience wealth. Feel the energy of abundance. Be the energy of abundance. Become one with wealth, abundance, and prosperity.

And now feel the energy of love. Unconditional love is in you and around you. Become one with unconditional love.

And now allow the energy of the universe to flow through you and around you and you become one with the energy of all. You are pure energy. You are pure positivity. You are pure possibility. You are the miracle.

Success Stories

I want to share a few successes that others have shared with me after using this material. I hope you have a few of your own to add here as well. Here is what others are saying:

"I have manifested the relationship I've been wanting with the opportunity to do income producing business with my loving partner. So very, very happy!"

"Manifested the relationship, wow!"

"Dear Joe, I love all you've taught me. I've gone from skeptic to doing a lot of divine work this week. My wife thanks you too."

"Manifested a showing of my photos in a gallery and sold four to five pieces..."

"It's been an amazing journey. So much has changed over the last few weeks. Life can never be the same. Looking forward to all the miracles coming my way!"

You are right; life can never be the same. You know why it can never be the same? Because you are no longer the same. All of these six lessons have put you in a different space. We're all in a different place of mind now. Even for me—this has helped me crystalize what I do and what I teach and has brought me closer to the miracle of the moment.

You know, in order for me to put my ego aside and ask for divine inspiration to come in and write to you, I have to step out of the way. I've got to have trust. I've got to have faith. I have to deepen my own connection to Divinity in order to be here now and serve you.

So, life is never the same, but isn't that great? Because life is miraculous! We're expecting miracles, we're living miracles, and more and more are coming all the time. *This* is the miracle.

Common Questions

Now I would like to share a few questions that others have had at this step in their process. I hope the answers will bless you as well.

There are so many layers of limiting beliefs that we need to unfold. How do we know when we have reached our true self? How do we know when we are fully awake and can follow our life's purpose and passion?

Well, I'm not trying to be funny here, but the best way to know is that you won't ask that question. I mean that if we're still asking, "How do I know when all my beliefs are cleared?" then we know all our beliefs aren't cleared yet. If we're still asking, "How do I know when I found my life purpose and I can follow it?" then we still haven't followed our life purpose. If we're still asking,

"How will I know when I'm awakened or I've sensed awakening?" then we know we're still not awakened.

The truth of the matter is we all have work to do. There is so much data, which is the term Dr. Hew Len used, that's in our unconscious mind that we have work to do. The good news is, as we're cleaning, we get closer and closer to *The Miracle*, to this moment, and we get closer and closer to the awakening. We get closer and closer to the witness that's behind everything that's going on.

We want to cheerfully march forward. We want to be a spiritual soldier in this army of awakening and we know that as we continue to do this, it'll get easier. It'll get lighter. You know, I went from being homeless and in poverty to, today, being more of a spiritual teacher than anybody, including me, ever thought, but it's only because I've done all that clearing work on myself over all these decades.

And I'm still cleaning, I'm still clearing, and I'm still doing this because I know how important it is for me to get to permanent awakening. I've had glimpses of awakening. I've had the satori experience, which is when you pretty much experience awakening as kind of a burst and you have a window that you see it and feel it but it's not permanent. We all want the permanent awakening.

How long does the awakening last for and is there anything I can do to stay awake?

Once you are awakened you stay awake. There is no going back from awakening. You stay awake. You don't have to worry about staying awake. You will be awake, because once you are awake—*you are awake*.

Awakening is unlike the other stages; if you've been a victim, when you go to empowerment, you could slide back. That's why I stressed that you want to remind yourself that you're no longer a victim. You know how to empower yourself, but you can slide up and down those first three stages of awakening. You can go into surrender and you can practice Ho'oponopono and one day you might feel like a victim and you'll slide back to the first stage of awakening.

That's when you want to remember this book, all the tools, everything I taught you, and everything we've shared. Use this to get back into empowerment and to get back into surrender. But when you awaken, you awaken for good. Once Buddha awakened, for example, he didn't go back to being unawakened. He was awakened. You can have glimpses of awakening but that's not awakening. Once you're awakened, you don't have to worry about it, you're there.

How do you know if you are acting out of inspiration instead of intention? Even if you are acting to help others, you may still be strengthening your ego.

Great observation, you are absolutely right. So how do you know if you are acting out of inspiration instead of intention? The first thing is you don't always know with great clarity. There are two or three ways to check yourself.

1. *The Silva Mind Control Method* by Jose Silva. Jose Silva is long gone, but his course is still around. He said any goal or intention you have should influence at least three other people besides you, and I think that's a good litmus test. It's a good rule of thumb. So if you have an intention or an inspiration and you're wondering if it's really an inspiration, you can ask yourself, "Is it helping other people beside me?" Then if it is, it's probably an inspiration.

2. Dr. Hew Len said that whenever he got an inspiration, he would check it by cleaning on it three times. What he meant by that is he'd receive an inspiration and then he'd wonder to himself, "Huh, I wonder if that's an inspiration or is that my ego tricking me?"
Then he would go, "I love you, I'm sorry, please forgive me, thank you" and he'd basically be praying to the Divine to say, "Show me if this is the way or not." After

doing that three times, if the inspiration was still there, he would go, "Okay, that's probably an inspiration; I will follow through."

Then in my own case, I look for the energy. If there is more of a blissful, excited, whole body energy that's coming from in my heart area, then I think, "Oh, that's an inspiration."

If I get an excited idea and it feels like it's up in my head, like it's a good idea and my thoughts are up in my head so the good idea is there too, it's probably an intention that's from my ego. That doesn't mean it's bad. Our egos are here to help us steer through life, otherwise we'd walk into walls, we'd do a whole lot of things inappropriately, and we wouldn't get along with other people in society. So the ego is here to help us. It's not necessarily a bad thing, and intentions aren't necessarily bad. I think it's preferable to have inspiration and you want to make yourself open to it. This is a great question because you want to verify to the best of your ability whether it's inspiration. Bottom line is you may not know for sure. You have to take your best, most faith-based choice, and then act.

I was very ill. I was diagnosed with a chronic heart failure disease and now I feel so great, almost completely healed. I was a zero when I started [this process], now I am a ninety.

Holy smokes, major applause; good for you! I'm proud of you. I send you more love. I'm telling everybody that these kind of miracles are what happen when you participate with this kind of awakening, with these kind of tools and exercises and processes.

It doesn't matter what's going on in your life, anything can be healed, and anything can be handled. I don't know that there's anything impossible. I don't know that there's anything incurable. We may have to work on ourselves, find a way, create a way, but I believe it's possible. Expect miracles, that's what this is all about, *The Miracle*.

Thanks to you, I am finally manifesting money. Yesterday I made $222 in one day and today I received $1,800 and it's just the beginning. I also like your song, "The Hook," a lot.

Oh, thank you very much. Complimenting my music makes my day. I love that you love the song, "The Hook," that's one of my favorite songs, and it's on my album, *One More Day*, which you can get on iTunes and other places. I sing it inside every time I feel I am getting irritated or angry.

You're manifesting money and that is a big thing. I say it's a big thing because so many people have had problems with it in the past, and because of these *Six Steps to Enlightenment*, you're getting through it, as is everybody else. It doesn't have to be a problem at all, but manifesting $222 and then $1,800 is a big deal, congratulations.

You have written so many books, could you share the top three of your books that mean the most to you and are most inspiring for others?

I'm glad to do it. It's a great question and a flattering question.

Zero Limits, the first book I wrote about Ho'oponopono, is hands down one of the few books that I've written that I re-read. I love that book. I feel like I dictated it from the Divine. I kind of channeled it. I didn't feel like I wrote it. I got it done in a couple weeks. It moved so easily. It just felt like it was inspired. I love the book, I love the story, and I want a movie made of it.

So if anybody reading this has movie connections, I want a movie made of *Zero Limits* or the follow-up book, *At Zero*. That whole story of Dr. Hew Len in the mental hospital, we've got to put that out there for the world to see. So *Zero Limits* would be my first choice.

The Attractor Factor, the book that got me into the movie *The Secret*, that'd be my second choice, because that has helped more people than anything I wrote up to that time. It is the number one bestseller out of everything I've written. It even beat *Zero Limits*. *Zero Limits* is incredibly popular, but *The Attractor Factor* is the number one bestseller out of all my books. If you haven't read *The Attractor Factor*, I would read it.

I'm proud of the book *The Secret Prayer* and I would recommend it, but I'd also have to say I wrote a book on P.T. Barnum that's called, *There's a Customer Born Every Minute*, and it's kind of a surprise. It's a very entertaining read and it's business oriented, but P.T. Barnum was mystical. His friends even called him Reverend Barnum. I wrote about his ten rings of power, the ten things he did for success, and one of them has to do with spirituality and his great faith. So I'd recommend those books, *Zero Limits, The Attractor Factor, There's a Customer Born Every Minute*, and *The Secret Prayer* I have to mention because it's a recent book and I'm proud of it.

We've Come a Long Way

I want to say a few things. First of all, I'm proud of you. I am grateful for you. We have gone the distance. Six lessons we've done together. We have done it. We have expected miracles, we have created miracles, and more miracles are to come.

Of course, I thank myself, and I thank Divinity for coming through and guiding me so I could be of the most use to you. I love you. I love you and I'm grateful for you.

Remember, *The Miracle* is right now. This is *The Miracle* and you are *The Miracle* and we are living *The*

Miracle. It's already here. Meanwhile, the new mantra in life is *Expect Miracles*. Thank you. I love you.

BONUS MATERIAL

Inner Child Meditation

As a bonus to help you release negative blocks for receiving all that you want to do, be, and have, I'd like you to have this Inner Child Meditation. Guitar Monk Mathew Dixon and I recorded this meditation in a downloadable audio that you can find at http://guitarmonks.com/innerchild/. You can either go get the audio (which has a beautiful, original score along with the guided meditation), or you can read through it here and follow along, or you can read and record it for yourself to use over and over. Either way, use this meditation as a healing tool to keep you connected to the Divine.

Let this be an easy process. You're just relaxing. You'll feel your body loosen up. You will allow the chair or the bed to support you as you let go. There's nothing to focus on but this moment and my voice. In self-identity Ho'oponopono, the mother is the conscious mind and the child is the unconscious mind. And what most of us try to do is run the unconscious mind by telling it what to do, yet the conscious mind knows very little about your life and even less about what's in the mind of the child or the unconscious.

Now that you've relaxed, your eyes are closed, somewhere in your being, imagine the child appearing. You don't have to visualize it. You don't have to describe it. Just let the child be there. And the very first thing you want to do is acknowledge the child. Simply look into the child's eyes and say, "I love you. I love you. I love you."

This child is holding all the memories and programs in your life. It has pain. It has hurts. Tell the child, "I'm sorry. Please forgive me." You may have had no idea how much the child hurts until now. It has accumulated memories. Those memories are programs that are running in your life right now. They don't all serve you, yet the child has not been acknowledged before. Acknowledge the child by saying, "I love you" repeatedly. "I love you. I love you. I love you."

And let the child know that you're truly sorry. That you've not paid attention to it before. Tell it, "I am sorry. Please forgive me" for neglecting you. "I am sorry."

Now ask the child for permission to pat it on the head with love. You must ask permission. You don't want to frighten the child. It is being heard, it is being loved. It knows you are there now. Softly reach out, and slowly, gently stroke the top of the child's head, saying, "I love you." Know in your heart that this is the most important relationship you can have in the world. Most of us spend

Inner Child Meditation · 287

our time looking for relationships outside of ourselves, yet once we heal the inner relationship with our child, the outer relationships become heavenly. They work.

But tell the child you love him or her and you're teaching the child how to love, how to receive love, as well as how to clear the programming that is in the child. By saying you're sorry for having been neglectful or even manipulative, you let the child know it is loved.

Now ask the child for help. Choose any problem that's going on in your life right now. That problem is simply a program in the child. It's a problem of perception and the child can release it for you. Say to the child, "If you don't mind, help me let go of the pain that's in you. Let us both release the memories and set ourselves free." And look at the child with unconditional love, truly feel this love as you say, "I love you," and as you say, "Please forgive me," and as you say, "I'm sorry."

And be sure to thank the child. "Thank you for letting me love you. Thank you for releasing the memories that were harbored in you. Thank you for healing yourself which heals me."

Now, ask the child if you may hug it. Again, you want to ask permission. The child will always say, "Yes," but you must not assume that and you must not take action until the child says, "Yes." So ask to hug the child, but not a scary hug. Not a bear hug, but a very gentle cradle. A very warm embrace. One that is pure love, feels all love, and gently put your arms around that child, embracing it. The child can feel your honesty.

And now you can even do another inventory for any other problem that may be in your life. It could be a health problem, a relationship problem, a mood issue, a financial problem. Whatever is there, ask the child to help you release the memory to erase this problem—to clear it, to cleanse it, to release it forever. All problems are our memories playing out within the child within you.

Let the child release those memories. As they are released in the child, they are released in you. This is how important the child is in your life. "I love you. I love you. I'm grateful for you. Thank you for being here with me. Thank you for being a part of me. I am so sorry that I've not paid attention to you before. Please forgive me for being unaware. Please forgive me for not paying attention to you. Thank you for healing yourself and me. Thank you for releasing all of these programs and memories. Thank you for loving me in return."

Now, as you relax with this inner child, give it a moment to give you any sort of message that it wants to say right now.

Accept whatever the child says. Thank it. Hug it in that warm embrace and say, "Thank you." Your inner child now knows how to do cleaning and clearing for you, and you now know how to make contact with the inner child.

You can do this inner child meditation every morning and/or every evening and throughout your day you might close your eyes and take a moment, connect to your inner child to ask it for any help or any cleaning. For now, just say "Thank you." Release the inner child so it can be with you, and in you, but on its own. Look at it with love and say, "I'm so sorry. Please forgive me. Thank you. I love you. I love you. I love you. I love you."

And now you can either drift off into a restful sleep or a nap, or you can awaken looking around the room, knowing where you are. Ready to proceed with your life with love, knowing your inner child is with you—cleaning and clearing and loving you every moment of every day.

Thank you.

Bibliography

Atkinson, William Walter. *Thought Vibration, or The Law of Attraction in the Thought World.* Chicago: New Thought Publishing, 1906.

Audlin, Mindy. *What If It All Goes Right?* Garden City, NY: Morgan James Publishing, 2010.

Barret, Daniel, and Joe Vitale. *The Remembering Process.* Carlsbad, CA: Hay House, 2015.

Behrend, Genevieve and Joe Vitale. *How to Attain Your Desires.* Garden City, NY: Morgan James Publishing, 2004.

Bure, Candace. *Reshaping it All: Motivation for Physical and Spiritual Fitness.* Nashville, TN: B&H Books, 2011.

Callahan, Roger. *Tapping the Healer Within: Using Thought-Field Therapy to Instantly Conquer Your Fears, Anxieties, and Emotional Distress.* New York, NY: McGraw-Hill, 2002.

Fox, Emmet. *The Mental Equivalent.* Life Summit, MO: Unity, 1932.

Goddard, Neville. *Neville Goddard Lecture Series.* 12 vols. Albuquerque: Audio Enlightenment Press, 2014.

Hill, Napoleon. *The Law of Success in Sixteen Lessons.* Blacksburg, VA: Wilder Publications.

Hill, Napoleon. *Think and Grow Rich.* New York: Fawcett Books, 1935.

Holmes, Ernest. *The Science of Mind.* New York: Tarcher, 2010.

Lawrence, Brother. *The Practice of the Presence of God: the Best Rule of a Holy Life.*

Larson, Christian D. *Just Be Glad.* Los Angeles, California: The New Literature Publishing Company, 1912.

Larson, Christian D. *The Great Within* (1907), CreateSpace, 2012.

Maltz, Maxwell. *Psycho-Cybernetics.* New York, NY: Pocket Books. 1969.

Ortner, Nick. *The Tapping Solution.* Carlsbad, CA: Hay House, 2013.

Silva, Jose. *The Silva Mind Control Method.* New York, NY: Pocket Books, 1978.

Vitale, Joe. *Attract Money Now.* Wimberley, TX: Hypnotic Marketing, 2009.

———. *The Attractor Factor; Five Easy Steps for Creating Wealth (or Anything Else) from the Inside Out.* Hoboken, NJ: John Wiley & Sons, Inc., 2006.

———. *At Zero: The Final Secrets to "Zero Limits," The Quest for Miracles Through Ho'oponopono.* Hoboken, NJ: John Wiley & Sons, Inc., 2013.

———. *The Awakened Millionaire.* Hoboken, NJ: John Wiley & Sons, Inc., 2016.

———. *Healing Music.* Wimberley, TX: Hypnotic Marketing, 2013.

———. *Instant Manifestation: The Real Secret to Attracting What You Want Right Now.* Portable Empire Publishing, 2011.

———. *Life's Missing Instruction Manual.* Hoboken, NJ: John Wiley & Sons, Inc., 2006.

———. *Miracles Manual. 3 vols.* Wimberley, TX: Hypnotic Marketing. http://www.miraclesmanual.com.

———. *The Secret Prayer.* CreateSpace: 2015.

———. *There's a Customer Born Every Minute: P.T. Barnum's Amazing 10 "Rings of Power" for Creating Fame, Fortune, and a Business Empire Today—Guaranteed!* Hoboken, NJ: John Wiley & Sons, Inc., 2006.

Vitale, Joe, and Daniel Barrett. *The Remembering Process.* San Diego: Hay House, 2014.

Vitale, Joe, and Dr. Ihaleakala Hew Len. *Zero Limits: The Secret Hawaiian System for Wealth, Health, Peace, and More.* Hoboken, NJ: John Wiley & Sons, Inc., 2007.

Wattles, Wallace. *Financial Success Through Creative Thought or The Science of Getting Rich.* Holyoke, MA: Elizabeth Towne, 1915.

Discography

Dixon, Mathew, and Joe Vitale. *Attract Money Now Meditations.* Audio recording. http://guitarmonks.com/amnm/

———. *The Enlightenment Audio.* Audio recording. http://guitarmonks.com/enlightenment/

———. *Fourth Dimension Meditation.* Audio recording. http://thefourthdimensionmusic.com/

———. *Inner Child Meditation.* Audio recording. http://guitarmonks.com/innerchild/

———. "I AM Prayer," *Invoking Divinity*, 2015, music album. http://guitarmonks.com/invoking-divinity/

Vitale, Joe. "Got a Problem?" *Strut!*, 2012, music album.
———. "Deep Within," *One More Day: Life Lessons in Hypnotic Song,* 2015, music album.
———. "Feel it Real," *One More Day: Life Lessons in Hypnotic Song,* 2015, music album.
———. "Some Thoughts," *One More Day: Life Lessons in Hypnotic Song,* 2015, music album.
———. "The Hook," *One More Day: Life Lessons in Hypnotic Song,* 2015, music album.
———. "The Secret Prayer," *The Secret Prayer* at *www.TheSecretPrayer.com,* 2014, audio recording.
Vitale, Joe, and Brad Yates. "Money Beyond Belief." Audio program. Wimberley, TX: Hypnotic Marketing, Inc.

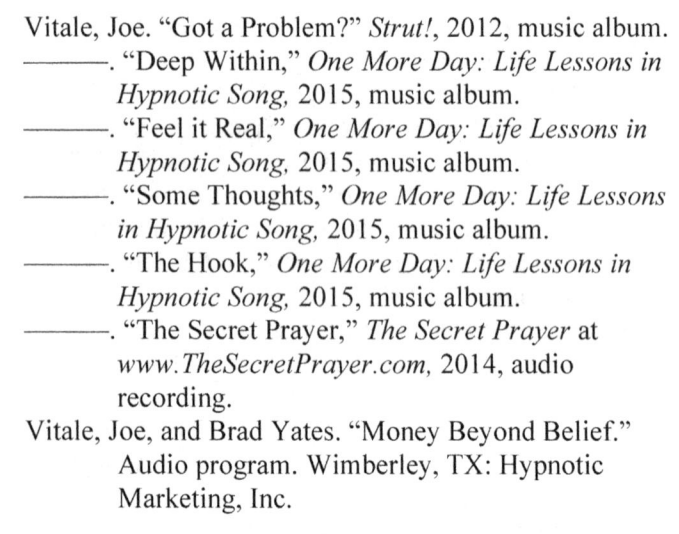

About the Author

Dr. Joe Vitale—once homeless but now a motivating inspirator known to his millions of fans as "Mr. Fire!"—is the world renown author of numerous bestselling books, such as *The Attractor Factor, Zero Limits, Life's Missing Instruction Manual, The Secret Prayer, Attract Money Now* (free at www.AttractMoneyNow.com), and *The Awakened Millionaire.*

He is a star in the blockbuster movie *The Secret*, as well as a dozen other films. He has recorded many bestselling audio programs, from *The Missing Secret* to *The Zero Point*. He's also the world's first self-help singer-songwriter, with fifteen albums out and many of his songs nominated for the Posi Award (considered the GRAMMYs of positive music).

He created *Miracles Coaching®, The Awakening Course, The Secret Mirror, Hypnotic Writing*, and many more life transforming products. He lives outside of Austin, Texas with his wife, Nerissa, and their pets.

His main website is www.JoeVitale.com

Join the Awakened Millionaire Movement
http://www.awakenedmillionaireacademy.com

Follow Dr. Joe Vitale:
Twitter: https://twitter.com/mrfire
Facebook: https://www.facebook.com/drjoevitale
Blog: http://blog.mrfire.com/

SPECIAL BONUS

Special Miracles Coaching® Offer

For the past twenty-five years I've been helping people like you attract ALL kinds of miracles in EVERY area of their lives.

I've helped people attract...

Money • Cars • Soul Mates • Better Health
New Careers • Dream Homes

The list goes on and on! And I can help you do the same in my Joe Vitale's Miracles Coaching® Program! The key is for you to be ready. (And it looks like you are or you would not be reading this right now.) If you want to learn more about how you can attract money, jobs, health, love, careers, relationships, or anything else quickly, and you want to sign up now, just go to...

www.miraclescoaching.com

Made in the USA
Monee, IL
06 September 2019